Messages
From
Mikela

50 Spiritual Doorways
To The Divine Inside You

Otto Collins

Published by Conscious Heart Publishing
P.O. Box 14544
Columbus, Ohio 43214

Paperback ISBN: 978-0-9725130-2-9

"From here on out...

Honor the sacred and the Divine in everything and every moment.

Get quiet. Notice your energy and let that be your guide for what to embrace, what to choose, what to say YES to, what to lay down, and what to say no to."

Mikela

INTRODUCTION:

About this Book and these Messages from Mikela

In the early part of October 2024, I began a practice that changed my life.

This practice is called a "Two-way Prayer."

I learned about it from the author and spiritual teacher, Elizabeth Gilbert, as I listened to her being interviewed by Tim Ferriss on his popular podcast.

On the podcast, Liz talked about something called a "Two-way Prayer" that she had begun some 20 years ago. As I recall, she talked about how it had affected her, had changed her life and kept her steady during turbulent times. It kept her focused on what was truly important and kept her sane in both good and bad.

In other words, this simple practice of a "Two-way Prayer" was life-changing for her.

I thought that if this was so powerful and so amazing for her, I'm going to try it.

And try it I did.

A few days later, late in the evening around midnight, I sat at my computer's keyboard and began the process of asking the same question that Liz starts her "Two-way Prayers" with:

"Dear Love, what would you have me know today?"

My interpretation of the way Elizabeth Gilbert described the "Two-way Prayer" is that it is different from your typical prayer that is "one way."

A "One-way Prayer" is you making a request and asking for something of the Creator, Source, the Almighty, Abba, the Universe or any other name you might choose for God.

A "Two-way Prayer" is you reaching out and asking a question of the great Spirit, the Divine or God and listening for a response.

Liz Gilbert began using the word "Love," which is what she thought a higher power should be all about, in place of the word "God" because it was a trigger word for her.

Personally, I have no problem using the word "God," "The Great Spirit," or any other word that may be used to describe the Creator.

I use the word "Love" in most of my prompts because my wife, Susie, and I have been writing, teaching, and sharing our ideas about love and relationships for well over twenty years and it just feels good to me to use that word.

I used it that first evening while doing my first "Two-way Prayer" and I had no idea what, if anything, would come when I asked this question, but the messages did come.

They came immediately and the messages were profound.

They were not only profound for me but they have been profound for everyone who I have read them to or shared them with.

Although these messages have been given directly to me, almost like a download from Spirit, they are universal in tone and spirit and are easily applicable to anyone's life who's open to exploring life in all its many colors and flavors.

The messages are simple, spiritual, and life-changing.

I haven't done this practice every night since I began, but I have done it most evenings and now have well over 50 messages and counting that have been given to me to help me in my life and to share with the world.

It's interesting that the messages I have been getting appear to originate from some place other than me.

Individually and together with my wife, Susie, I have written or co-written nearly 20 books and e-books over the years. The writing that began showing up on the page in these "Two-way Prayers" wasn't the way I normally write and the words were different words than I would ordinarily use in my writing.

These writings, or downloads, to me feel like something I've heard described before as "automatic writing" or even "channeled." After the first message was completed, "they" signed off the message with the name Mikela and that has continued ever since.

So, who or what is Mikela [muh-KAY-lah]?

I was curious about this myself and after about 30 messages or so, I asked that question.

The answer that came back to me was...

"Mikela is simply the spokesperson for the energies giving you these messages."

Call it my higher self, call it another being, call it my spiritual guides or call it a message from the great Spirit itself.

To me, the important part isn't the source of these messages. The important part is that the messages are so deep, so profound and so filled with truth and love that I can't keep them to myself anymore.

My guidance from the very beginning has been to share these messages and that's what I'm doing here.

In this book, I'm sharing 50 of the messages from Mikela and if you'd like to know more,

I'm happy to speak with you about them and their implications for you and your life.

How to Get the Most Out of These Messages and this Book

There will be some readers of this book who will wonder who is this Otto Collins guy and is he now an "enlightened" being and does he have his life completely together as a result of these messages flowing through him?

The answer to that is: Of course not.

I do not have my life completely together.

No one does.

I know, however, that I am an aspect of the Creator in human form.

I know that I am whole and complete and I can create anything from this place of wholeness.

I also know I am a highly sensitive person and while I can never know what challenges anyone else may be going through, I have certain unique physical, mental, and emotional challenges that quite often complicate my life.

As I see it, that is the beauty and power of these Messages from Mikela for me and for you.

Over and over and over again, these messages simply, lovingly and powerfully point the reader back to the truth of who and what they are at their core, at their essence.

Some of my questions that Mikela addresses are highly personal and require a great deal of vulnerability on my part to put them in the book.

At times, I wondered if it was wise to allow myself to "put it all out there" and allow these highly personal and important questions I was living with at a moment in time to be included in the book.

When I thought about this question, two things popped up for me:

One was the simple question of "Would including these highly personal questions and Mikela's answers be helpful to others?"

When I asked for guidance for the answer to that question, I immediately got back a resounding YES!

And the second question was "Should I wait until I am 'perfect' before I allow these deeply personal questions and Mikela's answers to show up in a book? "

The answer I got was that other people are struggling with the same things I've struggled with and they need the help now and not later.

So, I figure, if there is anything I can do to help people here and now instead of later, even if my ego gets bruised a little bit, I'm doing it now.

Plus, if I waited until everything was perfect before I allowed these highly personal questions to be addressed, we might be waiting a VERY long time.

What I know for sure is the answer I've gotten back from Mikela to any question I've had has brought me more peace, more understanding, as well as much more love for myself and others in all circumstances.

My Highest Suggestions for Getting the Most Out of This Book

The first thing I'll say is there is no right or wrong way to read this book.

Some people will choose to read the entire thing from cover to cover and other people will read a chapter a week and focus on that Message from Mikela for the entire week.

Others will choose to read the book through completely once and then skip around as they read a second time.

Other people, still yet, will find everything they need to get out of the book by simply opening to random pages or messages and seeing what is being shared at a moment in time, that, for them, is perfect for what they are going through or need help with in their life.

Sometimes I'll even play a little game and pick a random number between one and fifty and then open the book to that message. I usually find that the message I've chosen is exactly what I needed to hear in that moment.

In other words, you will find the perfect way for you to read this book and you will get exactly what you need from it in whatever way you choose to read it.

The Important Part

Even though the Messages from Mikela I'm sharing in this book are messages for me and to me, my suggestion is to read them as messages to you.

Read them about you, your life, your business, your health, your struggles with who and what you are, your beliefs that may be keeping you stuck, your personal challenges, and anything else you're facing in your life.

Read these messages as possibilities and opportunities for you and how you can choose to live and love from the highest point possible for you in this lifetime.

Please know, there are words and names in the messages I've never heard of and these were left in because that's the way they were given to me.

There are also "instructions" or "counsel" from Mikela that are counter to commonly accepted ideas, practices or ways of being or healing. We left them in the book because Mikela has clearly said to do very little editing, to present the book and the messages as they were given. My advice is to take what resonates with you and leave the rest.

My belief is that if it was included in one of the messages, someone, somewhere is destined to read or listen to them. When they read it or hear it, it will be extremely valuable and make perfect sense to them.

There is also something mentioned in these messages several times called "the Word." This doesn't necessarily mean being honest or being your word. The reference to "the Word" is about going through your moments, your day, and your life as if you are living consciously, from a place of being "Christ in action in all your words and actions."

I understand some of what Mikela says doesn't make any sense, appear like random thoughts or ideas completely out of place. Mikela says this is intentional and everything shared in these messages is "on purpose."

In other words, you'll get much more out of the book if you are focusing more on what's on offer for you in these messages and less time thinking about whether you should call the grammar police or not.

Most importantly, as you read these messages, read them SLOWLY.

You do not want to skip over the gold here and read through this book like the room next to where you are standing or sitting is on fire and you need to go put it out.

You're going to want to really take these messages in and let these messages simmer, stew, and marinate within you.

As you read, let yourself see what lessons, gifts, insights or takeaways are yours for the taking by simply slowing down as you read.

I feel strongly that if you will only open to what is being shared here in this book, these messages will have a profound and lasting impact on you and your life as much as they have mine.

Sending blessings and love,
Otto Collins

Table of Contents

Introduction: About this Book and these Messages from Mikela   v
Message #1   How to Start Your Day   1
Message #2   The Best Place to Ever Come From   3
Message #3   Creating a Healthy Body   7
Message #4   About Your Business   13
Message #5   Move It!   19
Message #6   This Is the Magic   21
Message #7   Talk More About Your Vision   25
Message #8   You are the Magician   29
Message #9   Time to Blow Off the Story   33
Message #10 Knowing the Truth   37
Message #11 Rip Off the Blankets   41
Message #12 Let's Start with You   43
Message #13 Beginning Again   47
Message #14 The Time is Now   51
Message #15 Start Now   55
Message #16 A Simple Suggestion   59
Message #17 You Are Being Chosen   63
Message #18 The Intersection Where The Magic is Made   67
Message #19 Worth and Divinity   73
Message #20 Stay   75

Message #21 Getting Healthy and Fit   79

Message #22 Equal to Anyone   83

Message #23 Your Feelings vs. "The Feeling"   87

Message #24 This is the Game   89

Message #25 The Meaning of Life   93

Message #26 The Secret Beyond All Secrets   97

Message #27 Choose Well   99

Message #28 Life as a Possibility Game   103

Message #29 A Love Affair with Your Body   107

Message #30 The Authenticity People Want   111

Message #31 The Place You've Been Running From   115

Message #32 No One Else's Path But Yours   117

Message #33 Two Ways to Live   119

Message #34 Living From the "Known"   123

Message #35 A Beautiful Obligation   127

Message #36 The Demands of Your Essence   133

Message #37 Mikela on Forgiveness   137

Message #38 Integrity and the Truth of What Is   143

Message #39 That's All It Takes   147

Message #40 Shine   151

Message #41 Would You?   157

Message #42 Required: A White-Hot Desire   161

Message #43 The Most Important Being That Ever Existed   165

Message #44 No Time for Playing Small   169

Message #45 One Thing You Should Never Deny   173

Message #46 Will You Invite It In?   177

Message #47 Test this Out   181

Message #48 A Beautiful and Sacred Act   185

Message #49 The Right Timing   189

Message #50 Loving Yourself   193

Acknowledgements   197

About the Author   199

MESSAGE #1

How to Start Your Day

Dear Love,
What would you have me know today?

The response:
I couldn't wait for this moment—the first moment of true surrender for you. I have been waiting for this your entire lifetime. I have been gently, lovingly, persistently guiding you toward loving yourself more and more each day.

I guide you to your soul's work and I guide you to your life's work and there's no difference. It's all God's work playing out within you, my Famous Butterfly.

I call you my Famous Butterfly because you are both soft and you like to fly away and this is both good and bad. It's good because it helps you see your beauty and it's bad because you allow yourself to be so easily distracted that it takes you away from your true gifts which are the gifts of loving, breathing into that love and seeing things as they really are and not how other people would like you (and the rest of the world) to think things are.

It's such a beautiful gift to be alive and it's painful to me to see you shut down your aliveness and live from fear, self-doubt and self-criticism.

But beginning today, I want you to know there is never a reason to be fearful. There is never a reason to be afraid. There is never a reason to not show up fully. And most importantly...there's never a reason to NOT show up as love.

I want you to know that no matter how much you've tried to shield yourself from the truth of who you are, it still shines through. It still bowls people over. But you hide it and you don't have to hide the truth of who you are any more.

I ask you gently, kindly and lovingly to commit to something right here and now.

Will you do it? Will you start your days and finish your days in love, in gratitude and in awe of the mystery of life?

Will you love yourself in the tough moments and the easy ones?

Will you love other people home?

Will you BE love to yourself and others?

Will you be the Word?

This is yours to do.

There's no reason to hold back. Ever. Now is the time. Now is the time. Now is the time to open your eyes and see you are the one chosen to come into this plane at this time and choose to live as love and choose to be free from fear.

There's never a reason to fear and there's always a reason to love.

I appreciate your willingness to open your heart even wider and find the space of love FOR YOU. Not for anyone else. For YOU.

And as you love you, you will love the world and you will be loved by the world in the most unusual of ways.

Be well my friend.

No fear. All love.

Be blessed (because you are.)

Mikela

MESSAGE #2

The Best Place to Ever Come From

Dear Love,
What would you have me know today?

It's so seductive to try to go at life alone. To feel like you got this, like you are the chooser and the hero, the decider and the mission driver.

No, it's not that way. Not that way at all.

It's ok, perfectly alright to take ownership of your greatness. What isn't alright is to think you are who is the decider.

This doesn't mean you can't decide the comings and the goings of your life. You can.

But it's the acceptance of the truth of who you are that allows you to see through the moments when you wish things were different only to find out that this IS your creation. This is your landing spot. This is your place where you heal, learn and grow. And what is so bad about this? NOTHING except for what you tell yourself is bad about THIS.

There is a place—let's call it a mountain where all is perfect, all is right and all is well.

That mountain is your "come from" place. It's your place of knowing. It is your place of seeing through the illusion that YOU... the "little you" have it all figured out.

You don't have to have anything figured out to enjoy this life and really experience happiness right where you are.

You'll notice I'm really big on you being right where you are?

That is because here, Now, Is the best place to ever come from as it relates to the medicine that ails you and many other people. The frustration of this lifetime which is wanting IT your way.

You came here to experience love, to be love and to believe in love.

Not just the romantic love, the stuff of lovers ripe with passion. But the lover who comes from love in ALL ways and sees this as his precious gift that can never be taken away.

I'll close with this for today.

Don't ever sacrifice who you are. Don't ever believe you are not the "chosen one." Don't ever believe you aren't here completely on purpose. Everyone is.

Embrace it now and burn it into your memory. You are the direct descendent of the mountain and the mountain is you. Paradoxical, I know. But you need to be training every day in the oxygen called love and life.

Live it. Breathe it in and don't ever think you aren't worthy because you are equal to the highest of the high. Surrender to the truth of who you are now.

No one ever dreams of the ordinary and you are not ordinary because you are here.

I embrace you in this moment from the energy field of "yunokwa"—the place of people and certainty inside you and inside us all.

Never fear. Always love.

Start with you and shine your light outward in the darkness and in the light.

Be well my brother, my soul friend and my wise man from above.

Heed the truth because it follows you everywhere.

Blessings and love to you this day.

Mikela

MESSAGE #3

Creating a Healthy Body

Dear Love,
What would you have me know about health and creating a
healthy body?

You are so magnificent, so young and so free that you are ingeniously creative (and stubborn).

You are so creative and so brilliant that you never get around to any kind of true commitment to true health.

Here's what I want you to know about health and how you can create your healthy body. Your healthy body, not anyone else's. Just yours.

I want you to learn about the healing properties of baking soda.

Once you do this, I want you to utilize this in a way consistent with a healing circle. I want you to learn what you discover about baking soda to stop you from eating anything that isn't healthy and doesn't serve you in creating your ideal body.

There's one other thing I want you to know. You can't "paper bag" yourself from the truth. You can't pretend it's not there. You can't wish life was different. You can't live in disharmony with nature. You can't fall from grace without any kind of consequences.

You MUST get this right. It is a true bargain to fill yourself up with ONLY the best, most nutritious foods.

You cannot live from a place of deceiving yourself. You can't hide from the truth. You can only wish you were someone who could live outside of natural law.

But you can't.

You have to decide how you are going to leap forward and choose the right way to move forward.

No more running from the truth. No more trying to deceive yourself in order to please the leftover voice that speaks to you when the spirit takes a pause and takes a breath and takes a break.

You are about to be asked to make a big change. Do not take the question or its answer lightly.

Make sure you are willing to see the truth and live from that truth.

No one can get away with what you have gotten away with for long. No one lasts forever and this is the biggest breakthrough for you—to see the truth of who you are and what is being asked of you.

Will you choose the brightest path that has been illuminated and prepared for you, or will you take the dark, deceitful path that knows nothing about your personal plan needed for healing.

It's time to go back and do EVERYTHING you can to live in complete and total surrender when it comes to food and drink.

There will be no more wishing. No more needing to break free. You are already free. There's nothing to be indebted to or indebted for.

You must be willing to take the high road and see and live only from the truth that you discover is YOUR truth.

You are asleep and it's time to wake up.

The spirit created the perfect system and the perfect way of being, eating and living and for some reason, you think your plan will prevail.

It will not.

Only health. Only love.

Love for you is doing what is best for you, not what is best for the voice in your head that cannot be trusted.

No more being chicken. No more letting your preferences run the circus. Seems pretty benign but time is important here.

One more strike and you're out.

It's not a game. It's life and its victory wanting to happen and waiting to be chosen.

Everything you want is on the other side of a healthy, trim, fit and athletic body.

It's time to bank on the only true source of wisdom. The only true source of guidance.

You can shift right now to the pleasure center of the universe.

You can make your decision based on love instead of blindness or weakness.

It's time to question every thought about health, fitness and freedom you thought you knew and sit in silence with the answers that are waiting patiently to show up and be counted.

Remember, your healthy body and your healthy mind are the cornerstone of the next phase.

You're WAY too smart to walk through life believing your own bullshit. You are a seeker of the truth (for you). And it's time to let go of all that other stuff.

Alkaline. Is the path. Make it alkaline and make it yours. Honor yourself and honor your Creator.

Love yourself and love your Creator.

Love your wife and love your Creator.

BE selfish about health. BE selfish about what is on offer. Don't settle for anything else that doesn't serve you in the greatest and most humble of ways.

Stay steady. Stay warm. Stay loving.

No more bullshit. No believing your dark voice.

Find every food that fits the definition of healthy for you and eat that, drink that and love that.

What you want, wants you.

Don't hesitate. Jump on the healthy human train. It's always and only one choice at a time.

What is loving?

When it comes to your fit, creative, healthy and happy body, shift 180 degrees.

Do it now.

What is loving? What is killing you? Get clear about that and live from that place.

Don't go back to sleep.

Wonder awaits.

Beauty awaits.

An even better life is yours.

Claim it now, oh wise one.

Volunteer to eat only love. Pray only love and be only love.

Surrender is the greatest act of love for you and for your connection to the Divine.

Nothing lasts forever. Keep that in mind.

Believe always in the good in you and the beautiful heart in you.

Blessings upon you, my ego-filled friend.

Nice to see you in spirit once again. Trust in the truth. And if you're wondering what the truth is, you already know the answer to that.

The truth is something that is still true when you stop believing in it. It's still true when the curtains come down and it's most certainly still true no matter the source.

Be easy on yourself. The truth is easy to see and hard to find in the "willingness soup."

I am your friend, your soul brother and your guide that breaks the rules.

Isn't it time you started living by the health and fitness rules that have always been true and will continue to be true?

But only Always.

Mikela

MESSAGE #4
About Your Business

Dear Love,
What would you have me know about my business?

Dearest creator of many things holy,

I come to you in this moment as a witness of someone committed to loving deeper and loving others.

There is a problem with your business that has gone unnoticed by you.

You're not making much money. And when I say it has gone unnoticed, I mean that at one level you have certainly noticed that the income for your business is not anywhere close to being a sustainable amount to pay your life expenses (let alone start to think about your business as a tool for the creation of abundance.)

What is missing is a clear, definite commitment to serving from a place of love. What's missing is a clear idea that you will do whatever is necessary to ring the bell of possibility for you and for others.

What is missing is a willingness to shout from the rooftops exactly how you want to serve, help and love people.

Your efforts are weak. Your efforts are about playing it safe. So far, your efforts are NOT spotlighting all that is on offer for another person's life by speaking with you, talking with you and connecting with you.

You have to deeply desire to serve and that is not happening.

Part of this is because you are tired, facing low energy much of the time, and are looking for a guarantee about how to make your ideas and your business successful in the way you want.

Have you ever considered how different your business would be (financially and otherwise) if you dropped every single ounce of fear, pain from the past and self-doubt about what you are "allowed" to create and experience in this lifetime?

The Great Spirit, AKA God, the Creator and the great mystery does not want you to fail. He or she wants you to live as the light of love in action. To live as the one who loves without condition. The great spirit is wanting you to be the one who sees and brings out the glory and the highest in others and that can only come when you and they are both opening and living from a place of loving truth and loving acceptance of the truth of who you are.

We have said to you earlier, there is never a reason to fear, and this is true. The trouble is, you don't seem to act on it in ways that break through the barrier of hesitation that keeps you from letting your light (and your message of love and hope) shine through.

This is something you are going to want to change. You are going to want to start showing all the people who cross your path the crazy, simple truth about the amount of love that is possible for anyone in this moment, in this day and in this lifetime.

If a person wants (and really deeply desires) a passionate marriage filled with the love-vibe uncommon in most households, then the message must be made clearer, more frequent and from a place of total love and honesty.

The business (your business) will be more successful when you are more successful at sharing the great news about the possibilities in the loudest, clearest and most humble of ways.

The business (your business) will be more financially successful when you claim that as a true desire and when your doubts and indecision is forced off the island of timeless success.

Want more clients? Be indispensable.

Be the one who is so attractive (not necessarily physically) in ways that others want to have more of what you have and more of what you talk about.

Shine the light on what is possible so often and so clearly that the other people you run across in life want not what you have but what's possible for them that you (and you alone) can point them to.

You have to do more pointing to possibilities and less holding back.

Less doubt, less judgment and less wishing things were different.

Life (and success) responds to a vision.

Do you have a vision and do you create daily and in each moment from that vision?

What do you want for yourself? And what do you want for the people you meet in your daily life?

You have to be clear about what you offer and to not ever be afraid to show people that there could be a gap between where they are in their love life and what is possible for them.

You have to be willing to ask more provocative questions to bring out a greater desire. You have to be willing to shout from the rooftops what you see that's on offer for them.

The problem is, you hold back and you doubt that others can have their version of what you have. But you can't do that and hope you will be as successful financially as you would like.

Additionally, this isn't about the money.

It's about serving and showing up as love in action to such a degree that other people start to notice the gaps and start wanting more. That's when your conversations will turn into more coaching conversations and more possibilities in the eyes of your brothers and sisters who will come across your path.

The key is this: Point to what's on offer that people can't see.

Point to what they want, but don't know they want it yet.

Help people to see that they don't have to lose themselves and who they think they are in order to have the most incredible love ever.

You have to take the idea of being bolder as the most loving act of kindness you could ever give. You have to believe in what you're selling.

Get really good at having conversations about the gap and the gain. And when I say this, I'm talking about the gap between where they are and what might be possible for them and to help them notice when life and love is getting better.

This isn't some esoteric jibber-jabber I'm saying here. I'm talking about the place to come from and the place you can speak from that will be received with a welcome and the desire for "more of that, please" from the people you meet in your life.

You have to trust in YOU, what is possible for your future and what can be possible when you simply trust in the power already within you that literally has been endowed with the seeds of greatness.

Be only love and spread only love and possibilities, one day and one moment at a time.

From now on, simply drop everything that doesn't lead to peace, love and freedom.

Abundance is everywhere, but the most important thing to know is that abundance is already inside you.

You need to start acting like it, because you already know everything you need to know to lead anyone to the highest and the best version of love ever.

So, go get started.

Love more. Love deeper. Love without compromise.

Share the possibilities.

With everyone you meet.

Start now.

Mikela

MESSAGE #5

Move It!

Dear Love,
What would most help me right now?

More exercise.

It's really simple. When a person gets down on themselves, and dare we say, even depressed and thinking that life hates them or they can't see their way forward—

They need to move.

Move your body.

Move it for 20 to 30 minutes with vigorous movement and then top it off with lifting the heaviest weights you can for 10 to 15 reps. DO the arms. Do the back, shoulders, biceps and wicked flys.

No time for whining around. Movement is the key.

Movement will change your attitude and your body.

Move it. Move it. Move it. Or lose it, lose it, lose it.

You asked, and now you know.

Movement is the key to being who you want to be.

Love is the answer. Movement is the key.

Blessed being.

You are amazing.

Love yourself. Never forget.

Until next time.

Mikela

MESSAGE #6

This Is the Magic

Dear Love,
What would you have me know today?

"I can't wait until the magic happens," she said.

"This IS the magic," responded the great one.

So often we think that the magic hasn't happened yet or we need to wait for the magic to happen or better yet, we have to do something to make the magic happen in our lives.

Well, here's the truth of it: The magic is already happening. It's happening in every single moment right in front of your very eyes, inside you and inside everyone.

What we are trying to say is, there's a gift that everyone is given when they are born and there's the gift that everyone dies knowing. There's a BIG difference between the two but the lesson is the key here.

You, your beloved, your friends, your family or anyone don't have to go anywhere to find the magic. It's only and always right here inside you.

No joke.

We get it that you and your brothers and sisters are both in awe, in fear of the magic that's always within, but there's no reason to strike the warning bell. There's no reason to be alarmed and there's certainly no reason to ever worry about tomorrow.

It will come and it will be exactly what it is supposed to be. Nothing more and nothing less, but that should never diminish any aspect of the awe and mystery that is the winder upper and the decider and the chooser of all things mysterious that are in essence the great unknown (at least to you and to us.)

You see, even we do not completely understand and recognize the beauty that exists within you and everyone.

You don't have to go anywhere or do anything to recognize and take ownership of the great gift there is which is...

The miracle and the truth.

The miracle is the absolute truth of who you are and the fact that who you are is always fresh, alive and making the next phase of life begin again and again and again as you see each moment as a possibility.

The truth is you are who you are, and you can deny it all you want, but the truth is you are who you are. You are who you claim you are even though that may not be who you really are.

Who you really are is an open, loving, fearless spirit walking among all the other spirits in such a way that you will one day be recognized as the ONE who cannot be less than who he is—who she is—as you lay all your burdens down and embrace the truth of who you are.

And this is a man who runs interference for himself as his god-self and as the one who is so crystal clear about who he is that others notice. Others take heed and others see the truth inside themselves.

What a light you are.

It is all about shining that light as brightly as possible and in the way that best serves you and best serves humanity.

No more slow-going.

It's time to wake up to the true nature of who and what you are.

And this is the rectifier and the believer. You are the rectifier of all fear in yourself and others who cross your path. And you are the believer of what you see and what has and what will be shown to you as a self-esteem and self-gratitude gift that allows you to be a way-shower and a way-seer.

Cut off everything that doesn't bring more peace, love and freedom to live into your truth and to live into the truth that is true always.

You are magnificent. You are sacred. You are divine.

You are a soul, full of light that never dies.

Farewell until the next time we chat.

Mikela

.

MESSAGE #7

Talk More About Your Vision

Dear Love,
What is the next right action in our business?

Dearest Otto,

We want you to know you are a gift to couples everywhere. We love how you and your mate are a shining example of two people who genuinely love each other and want to be together.

And it shows.

As far as your business, now is the time to start talking about your vision more and expressing it more and more out into the world.

It is time to be really clear about what you see that is possible for other men, women and couples that they can't (or won't) see for themselves yet.

Take, for example, the podcast you just did about true heartfelt love and connection—the one about how two people in a relationship or marriage could literally...

"Never fight or argue again."

This is really big because when you talk about this idea in your work of something called "never fight or argue again," you have just said something most people would find hard to believe.

In fact, it's something most people can't even fathom.

When most people hear you start talking about a marriage or relationship of any kind where fights, arguments and disagreements are nonexistent and there's still plenty of love, connection and even passion-- they begin to wonder,

"How is that even possible? After all, we disagree, argue and fight about everything!"

Then you're going to want to invite people into conversations about true heart connection that only gets stronger over time.

In other words, you're going to rock people's world with an idea of not ever fighting, arguing, and feeling disconnected again.

Then, it's going to be really smart to start a conversation about the three primary ways we keep love away...

Fight, Flight, or Freeze.

In other words...

Spend some time in your work talking about how people choose up sides and look for an enemy in their relationships and then wonder why they feel disconnected from one another.

Talk about how people withdraw themselves and how they withdraw their love when they don't have to and finally...

Spend some time talking to your followers about how they get frozen and get stuck and how this comes from a place of fear about the future based on their history and their past.

Otto, you yourself sometimes get frozen in your life and in your business because you are sometimes afraid to take a stand for you. And most tragically, you get stuck seeing ANY way forward that isn't painful.

No one should ever have to feel disconnected from someone they really care about.

Never.

And you can help people with this issue.

It's time to be a little (or maybe a lot) bolder in your work, and share more from your hearts and share from your experiences about what keeps love away (without people even realizing it.)

Bolder, kinder and from a place of love—that's the place to come from.

Let's get started.

It's time.

You can do this.

With Mega Love.

Mikela

MESSAGE #8
You are the Magician

Dear Love,
What would you have me know today?

Dear Otto, my favorite blossom in this moment, who is ready to blossom at any moment and shoot his vibrancy in all directions as he lays down his uneasiness about saying to the world and himself how much he is the Word in action and the Word in form as well as the Word in the energy fields that surround him as he walks his path of love.

Otto, you are a magician. Not to show off or impress others with tricks or parlor games, but you are a magician who is skilled at shortening the path for the non-believers to find their way home. You really are a magician.

And you can perform your magic in THIS lifetime as well as anyone. But you must believe that you can do it. What you are is a magician who is helpful and what you are called to do is in alignment with your soul's mission and path of healing and growth.

The magic you can perform is influence. Influence through love, through authenticity and through personal power–the kind of personal power that is always untouched by the personality or anything that is subject to the comings and goings of life on the earth plane.

You are much more of an influencer than you know in this moment.

Your words, your actions, and your being influence others for good and for eternity.

The necessary thing for you to remember in each moment of your days truly is that nothing lasts forever.

That alone should be enough to allow you to lay down any fear, any doubt or any hesitation toward saying YES and taking the next step forward and the next right action you are required to take in service to humanity.

Whatever you want should be built on a foundation of what is permanent and will never pass or fade away. This is the personal relationship with the one referred to in *The Way of Mastery* as "the Comforter."

In this moment, the number one thing we'd like you to know is the victim party is over. It's time to claim the truth of who you are.

You are one who sits in his divinity and serves.

And as you serve, the difference is clear and certain in the impact your words and your work have on the world.

We are not saying you will be a worldwide celebrity, as this will not be the case. We are saying your service will overthrow the madness and the false paradigms that the people who cross your path wish they could experience in this one beautiful lifetime.

In closing, what we would like you to know in this moment is how much of a magician you truly are.

Your magic comes alive as you serve.

It fades away when you don't.

Now is a perfect time to acknowledge, know and accept the truth of who you are.

No more gamesmanship, no more pretending you are not great and no more pretending you are not a magician.

Use your magic for good, my friend.

And as you say YES to doing this more and more of the time, you will be recognized in the spirit world as the one who says YES and the one who no longer needs anything. This is because he knows the truth that is true always. You already have everything you need. Right here inside you.

You are a divine being made of love and light sent here to heal, learn and grow and to help others do the same.

You cannot do otherwise, no matter what you choose for your life journey and your life path.

You are the magician.

Claim that now. Will you, please?

My blessings to you in this time and in this moment and for all time.

Mikela

MESSAGE #9
Time to Blow Off the Story

Dear Love,
What would you have me know today?

Dear Otto,

You are like a cinnamon biscuit. You are sweet and not much endurance.

You need to be the other way around. MUCH more endurance and only some sweet.

It's a free ride to the shore where the sun is, but there is something else on offer.

What is on offer is the experience of having many more tomorrows be the way you want instead of the way you don't want.

Here's a small lesson:

Take tomatoes, for example. You don't like tomatoes really, but you eat them anyway in tolerable amount and in the ways you have found that would work for you.

This is the master key for anything new that you want to expand in your life. There will be things you will encounter that you will not like and things you are going to have to start slow with but will be necessary to get used to.

These things are going to change your life.

You aren't going to like some things in life that will be really helpful and really valuable to you as you enter the next phase of your life and spiritual growth path.

Shake it off. Don't settle into a life of regret and disillusionment when you don't have to.

Taking the lead and taking the next step is life-affirming and can be a huge catalyst for your real work that is to come.

It's time to blow off the story that you can't do something you are perfectly capable of doing simply because you have allowed your story of "I'm this," "I'm that" or "I'm too" (fill in the blank) to do this.

Nonsense.

Just like it is in learning to eat tomatoes, you can learn to open yourself to anything that will be helpful to you on your path. You just have to see the possible victory on the other side in order for you to complete the task that's needed to be more of the true success you want.

And this is the key: Create the vision, decide what you want and then simply start putting one foot in front of the other to create what you want to create and to build the life you want to build (and this can be done quickly.)

Stop allowing the whiny little girl of a personality to run the show known as your life.

Take a step back and become so acutely and keenly aware of what you want and what the spirit wants to create through you that you can't help but be successful in creating what you want.

Start here and use the one-foot-at-a-time method to let go of the shame you are carrying and just create for your sake, for Susie's sake, for everyone's sake and most of all, for God's sake.

We've said this a lot to you in these past few days...

The time is now to create and express through this vision the very essence of who you are and what you bring to a conversation, a consciousness or a life craving more.

Start with your life. Begin there and throw away the filter of anything getting in the way of what is to be shared and what is to be lived in this new divine order called your life.

Be as purposeful, intentional and as loving as you can and start where it is needed most within and without you. Love you, accept you, appreciate you and welcome anything that begs for a welcome and a forgiveness.

No need to look to the past. It's all right here in your moving forward in the next big act—your freedom from your personal mind—the personality and the fears that tie you in place.

Let go of ALL fear, ALL history and ALL wishes that arrive with the baggage from the past.

Love is now. Love is now. Loving you is now the top priority.

Only do what is in support of you loving you and then reach outward to the world from there.

One moment at a time is all you can do, but the vision is the vision.

Make the vision so wonderful, so inviting and so worth it that it will pull you through ANYTHING instead of you feeling like you have to get out and push something that is not even yours to push.

Start with the new vision. Hold Susie's hand and go together.

Love yourself. That's where the power is in this.

Make this be much easier than you've been making it.

You deserve it.

You just make sure it's fun (and remember where fun comes from—you decide that too) and incorporate fun, play, and your highest wisdom into the mix or it's not worth doing.

The path is being laid out before you.

Just be a believer inside and a way-shower on the outside.

That is all for today.

Love yourself and give to yourself as you are loving and giving to others.

It's the only way. Otherwise, it's all out of balance and it won't work (this life of yours.)

Blessed be for this moment and for all times.

Your fellow spiritual traveler.

Mikela

MESSAGE #10
Knowing the Truth

Dear Love,
What would you have me know today?

Dear Otto,

You are an amazing soul who is getting this at deeper and deeper levels.

And what is the THIS you are getting?

The true essence of this plan...the plan for you and the plan for everyone. That's what.

You can try if you want. But, one day you are going to know and we mean *know* with a capital K-N-O-W what the purpose of your life and this incarnation is and you are going to be pleasantly surprised to learn what all the fuss has been about.

Start here.

For you and countless others, millions, perhaps, that are alive in this moment...

Your soul's learning in this moment and at this time is simply to know the truth and to know yourself.

To know the truth means to take the truth of who you are and live from that understanding day in, day out. And to "know yourself" is simply to know the difference between the soul and the personality.

The soul and everything it stands for, wants and is entrusted to be and live into is eternal. Meaning, it or the real you will never die, can never fail and can never be without worth in this moment or any other.

As for the personality, there is NOTHING about the personality that is permanent, everlasting or immortal and eternal. NOTHING.

With this knowledge, you can absolutely know what to pay attention to and what to take seriously and what to ignore and know it isn't real.

The soul is real and the personality is not.

The implications of this are not only enormous but life-changing when you consider the essence of this truth:

That there is NOTHING to ever fear, nothing ever to judge, and certainly nothing ever to hold back on if it is in alignment of your highest good.

To check in and know if we're dealing with something at the soul or the personality level, all you have to do is ask. That's right, ask.

Things born of the personality can be entertaining and fun and they can also be very painful.

Don't play the game of fear, ever.

Don't play the game of "I can't," "I won't," or "I wish I could."

Anything that is on offer from a soul-level and a soul perspective is always available. And sometimes attaining your soul desire can take a lifetime of healing and a lifetime of letting go of beliefs and untruths that would no longer serve you in any capacity, but you keep dragging them around anyway.

It's time to let go of anything that doesn't take you toward your soul's mission and say a full-bodied "YES" to all that can be seen as you look out at your possibility vista.

Once you check in with your divine source of knowledge within, you will always know exactly what to do.

Sometimes, it takes a while to open the doorways and get clearer about the next right move but the answers will always come. They come in perfect timing—your perfect timing. No sooner. No later.

My beautiful soul-friend...

Embrace the unknown for it is only unknown at the personality level. And as you know, the personality is weak and cannot be trusted to know truly what is best for someone like you. It's just an impossible thing (to know) without looking backward at a life well lived.

My beloved friend, do NOT scratch an itch that doesn't need to be scratched. Do NOT join hands with any path, any concern, anyone or anything that is not for your soul's highest good.

Take this seriously and see how much it makes a difference as you start moving forward with this new understanding that will be helpful on your life journey.

You will be amazed. You will be blessed beyond measure.

Focus on the truth and focus on your healing.

No more wishing. Only forward movement toward the path of the divine.

Bless you on your path. It is a holy one and a righteous one.

Remember always to lay any and all fears down.

Stay loving and stay kind.

Serve others from this place of true love and service.

The bounty awaits.

Mikela

MESSAGE #11
Rip Off the Blankets

Dear Love,
What would you have me know today?

Dear Amazing Otto,

Thank you for your service to your community and to humanity.

We are loving all the space you have opened up in your world for the next right thing.

And we say it is time to rip off the blankets and see how comfortable you can really be without the extra covers.

No more need for safety.

No more need for fixing up of your old ways.

No more bringing the old into the new world and wishing it wasn't there.

This message today is a very simple message.

Get the help you need to see life differently.

Open to seeing the truth about life, love and abundance.

One day none of this will matter.

One day all of this will matter.

Come from that place where both of those things are true.

Blessings and love to you, Roger.

Until next time...

Mikela

MESSAGE #12
Let's Start with You

Dear Love,
What would you have me know today?

Dearest Otto,

You are tired and you have to get some relief.

You have to focus on getting healthy and getting sane.

We say getting healthy because there is nothing that will gift you the energy you need more than lightening your load on your body.

It's very smart to slice off the extra weight that is causing you to have low energy and it's more than smart to lighten the load on your mental body.

Lightening the load on your physical body will produce results you can't even begin to think of right now.

You'll have more creativity. Your sparks in the brain will start firing more rapidly and with more efficiency. You'll remember things better and your ability to think clearer will return to near normal levels.

As far as the load on your mental body: While it's true that your physical body is what carries the soul around to do its work here in the physical plane, it's the mental body that needs the extra juice to breathe new life into your soul's work and your soul's calling.

We say all these things to say, YES, you have to work, earn money and save money. But what you really have to do is save your energy and build your energy up, up, up.

No doubt about it, the quest for freedom is going to get a big shot in the arm as you move in the new direction.

You need a job that allows you to serve humanity and serve the world while at the same time allows you to rebuild your energy to the point that you bring the heavens to you in your real-life desires and the level of service you are capable of in the world.

Let's see how the doors of possibilities can be swung open as you get your new marching orders.

Love yourself. Love others.

Feel the truth of what is being asked of you and what is being asked of you in the way of service.

There's nothing to be afraid of.

The comforter is always with you. The truth is always on your side. The best thing you can ever do is continue to ask for guidance and ask for help.

There's nothing you can't do as long as it's in alignment with your soul's current journey and your freedom to live in the light, and it brings you joy.

If it's not fun, don't do it.

Serve yourself. Serve your mate. Serve the one in front of you and serve the Creator.

It's time to claim your divinity. It's really hard to do that when your socks are wet and you can't find your way home.

It's always easier to find your way home when the batteries that run the energy stacks are able to be fully charged and fully engaged.

Let's choose love in every moment. Let's start with you.

And from there, you can shine your light outward and with the radiance that wields the spirit that sings instead of whines, that remembers instead of forgets and dusts himself off instead of staying stuck.

Make the most of every moment.

Fresh, clean and happy is the way, the place to come from.

Make the best from every moment and every interaction.

Love is always the starting place. Love has many different looks. Open for the wisdom and the guidance as you move forward.

This moment is important.

Never doubt the good you can create in the world.

Mikela

MESSAGE #13
Beginning Again

Dear Love,
What would you have me know today?

Dearest Otto,

You are the creator of the universe. You are the disciple who is learning to listen deeper to the one. You are becoming the one at peace, in fullness and in all ways related to living in the life you are choosing and the life chosen for you.

Let's begin again. Actually, you are beginning again. Starting right now, in this moment, as you are in all moments—you are beginning again.

The question is, what will you choose to begin again, or choose to begin for the first time.

There is no such thing as the past (except in your imagination) so this and everything you choose and everything that chooses you is something that is beginning fresh, alive and for your growth's sake in THIS moment.

It's time to put away the glasses you used to wear, for you cannot see with much clarity from the eyeglasses of old. You must wear the glasses you have prescribed for yourself and that have been prescribed for you.

As you can tell by our words, there are two things present right now that are both true. There is what is being created for you and there is what is being created by you. Both are important now and will become even more important in the coming days, weeks, months and years.

Dissect in an instant what you see around you and you will see the choices at hand that must be chosen by you, for this moment, for this day and for this life of yours.

Never again will you wonder whether you should do something or not. The dictates are coming in hot. In other words, the lessons you are here to learn are being given to you by choice point.

They are choice points due to the fact that you get to choose what will become of the wrecks known as your past and the residue from those past painful memories and decide once and for all what healing will take place in this Holy Instant.

Yes, THIS is a Holy Instant as are all moments "Holy Instants." A Holy Instant is a moment in time where you recognize, truly recognize, that THIS moment is HOLY.

And when you see a particular moment as Holy, you treat it as such.

It, therefore, serves as a reminder that if all moments are "Holy Instants" then all moments should be treated as such and should be revered by you as HOLY.

Does it change things if a particular moment is recognized as a "Holy Instant"?

Of course it does. But not any more than seeing the Divine in everyone and everything (and that includes seeing the Divine in you) as the starting point.

So, if there is anything that must be known, must be remembered and must be transformed it is the belief you have about who and what you are.

You are the Divine living in an earth body. You are the structure that wishes to be known but cannot be further known due to that fact that you, the real you, is already in the record books as a spark created to manifest in the infinite and the one known as the decider in this moment.

It's time as we have said before to count the moment you're living in to be the only one that's important. The only one worth considering and the only one that will matter as you take each step on your soul's journey of recognition in truth, in recognition of who you are.

And here's the best part and what we have been wanting to say to you up until now.

Live as if you are the manifestation of the Christ right here and right now because you are the one chosen and the one who chose to come forth as an extension of God's love in action.

No more sweating and no more plundering are the mantras of the day. Show up and show out as the wonderful beautiful creation that you are. As you do this and as you become this, you will see the changes more and more each day and in each thought made manifest as a choice in each moment.

Stop all fear games. Know and accept only the truth of who you are. For the truth of who you are is being made manifest right now, in this day and for all eternity.

Say goodbye to the old and say hello to the truth of who you are.

In love and in spirit is where we meet you.

Be well, my earthly friend.

Mikela

MESSAGE #14

The Time is Now

Dear Love,
What would you have me do in this job situation?

Dearest Otto—Our Main Man.

Sign us up for some serious fun.

C'mon, Otto.

This is your big moment to start your transition to the next phase of your career, your business and your life.

Isn't it lovely that you can now let all the "shoulds" go and rely on the fact that you will always be taken care of no matter what?

By this, we don't mean you're going to be sent a big canvas bag of cash in the mail that will suddenly be the gift that keeps on giving.

No, it's far greater than that.

You are being gifted the gift of freedom, of truth, of mercy and willingness to stand right where you are and make your next move from there.

What you've been wanting all along is here and it's been waiting for you. The problem is you haven't been truly calling it to you (as those manifesters say.)

You've been content to whine around and play small and hope the manna starts to flow your way without you making the first big move.

But, no more of that.

The corner has been turned and now you can say YES to the magic that waits for you on the other side of the news that you just received energetically. And that news is the fact that the world is done waiting for you to make your move and they are now (energetically) getting out their trumpets and sounding their collective horns to announce the arrival of the new you.

That's right, the new you is the one who is alive and has been gifted with the energy of the preacher who loves and the philanthropist who gives and the salesman who sells.

You are going to be moving forward in loving and miraculous ways to open hearts to the many who can't yet see the beauty of love on their doorstep they haven't been willing to invite in.

What a blessing it will be to the ones entering your energy field who need an old- fashioned love shower of possibilities delivered in a new way that they can now see and be open to.

The time is limited for you to make this transition. You have been waiting for the just right, very perfect moment to claim your divinity, but that is long since passed.

There is no more time for others to do the work you are meant to do. It's not right to hope others will be called as you have been called to radiate your greatness into the world as only you can do.

Now it is perfectly clear. The time is now to clear the decks of anything and everything that will get in the way of your perfect rising to meet the occasion.

No more wishing for something that is not yours to have.

It is time for the flash to happen and the dream to commence and most importantly, it is time for you to say a full bodied "YES!" to what is taking place with or without your conscious action.

The stars have aligned and the timing is right for you to ring the bell that signifies your willingness and your readiness to open the new gate and blow the winds toward those who need your particular message of hope.

Remember the truism you have heard many times before now that is so very true in this moment. "The universe is conspiring on your behalf to bring only good to come to you and through you."

Even those things that could be viewed as "bad news" can only be seen as good news when the spotlight of wisdom is shown on them. It is so easy to walk away from the known and walk away from insanity when you know who walks beside you. And those people and those beings we are referring to are truly on the right side of this transition, and they support you and they love you.

You are waking up to the possibilities that have always existed for you but you were not quite ready for. Now you are ready.

Now you are clear about the truth of who you are (and how you serve).

The faucets are about to be turned on, and you will be the one who will be turning them on as you step deeper and deeper into your soul's contract and your mission in this lifetime.

There is no reason to wait any longer.

Let your ministry begin anew. Let it begin for real. Let it be the manifestation of all the days messages to come. And those messages are the dream into reality that all men long for.

Let your life be lived from this moment on from a place of love, strength and integrity.

Love for each other. Strength for what is needed and integrity to live in communion with your highest good and what will serve from the highest point of the cylinder.

Love all. Love as one. Let love come forth.

The dreamer of the dream has arrived. And his name is Otto.

It's time you let go of the old and start acting like the dreamer, the lover and the manifester that you are.

Happy trails to you.

With love as your template, go forth.

We're wishing you smooth laughter and no tears as you embrace the highest of the high in your travels.

Mikela

MESSAGE #15

Start Now

Dear Love,
What do you want me to do next in my business and in my
business with Susie?

Dearest Otto,

The time has come to start letting people know what is on offer. And by what is on offer, we mean that it's time for people that enter your energy field (even for a moment and even from a distance) be shifted in some way by your presence and by the proclamation of what is on offer for their one precious life.

Yes, all life is precious and there has to be an opening, a small gap through which you can enter into in the hearts and minds of others without the fear trigger going off for them that there is something to be protected and something to be feared by stepping into the unknown and the previously thought of what is unattainable or impossible.

Begin with a positive offering, a stance that you can take that seems like a crazy creation and something without ties to the past that when people hear it, they go, "I want that!"

Connect to what people want. They want freedom, they want love, and they want to have permission to claim their divinity. To make it ok to want what they want.

What would be a stretch for people in the love that they really want, but don't think they can have?

What would bring true happiness in all aspects of life?

What would people pay for that they don't know is that important that they would give ANYTHING and any amount of money to create, have or be THAT?

In short, they would pay ANYTHING you ask if you could just tap into the unfulfilled story living inside their head.

It's like Joe Vitale once said: That you enter into the story already going on in their head and you lead them into a new, more powerful story they want and up until now, haven't been able to step into.

The genius of this is that you are essentially giving people what they most want in this lifetime.

You have too much integrity to play to people's fears, doubts and insecurities, but something you MUST do is have them climb the ladder and look over the horizon to the beautiful possibility calling to them that will not leave them alone and won't go away.

Our simple suggestion is to start offering groups online where you really go deep and give people a true taste of their most important desires (especially the unspoken ones.)

The bolder the claim that is held in truth is what is being called for here.

Take the first step as soon as you can.

Invite, connect, claim your divinity and welcome your brothers and sisters to the party within them they truly long for.

It's time for bolder action taken from a state of grace and from the power of a love not realized yet.

Ripe is what people are to your unique message.

They are ready for the shifts and the changes that have been percolating within them.

It's time to help them eat the fruit of their choosing.

It's time to make people much more aware of the possibilities they can't see yet.

Let the transformations begin.

Let the special needs of the ones attracted to you come forth in miraculous ways.

You are not drunk and you are not staggering around. You are a leader who leads people home to the love they are and the love they are capable of.

Start with BIG FAT LOVE and work outward from there.

Remember, this is NOT the time for fear. This is the time for love being offered in word and in deed.

No more fear. No more polarizations. No more wishing you had what was on someone else's plate.

It's time to metaphorically make more music and share more of you two and of the possibilities.

Stop lying to yourself that you don't know what to do.

When you show up as the embodiment of love, the rest is easy.

Start now.

Get going.

Plan something now.

Do it now.

With as much love as we can offer.

Come from the feeling of relaxed possibilities.

There's no stretching going on here because you are THIS already.

All you have to do is be willing to shine the light of possibilities on everyone who crosses your path.

Yours in the Holy situations that open hearts to new possibilities.

Welcome home.

Mikela

MESSAGE #16
A Simple Suggestion

Dear Love,
What would you have me know today?

My Dear Child Otto--

You are the brightest in the box. You are beauty in disguise and love everywhere you turn.

The most important thing we would have you know today is everything is going to be all right. In fact, it's not going to be all right. It's already all right. You just feel at such a depth that you get overwhelmed and overwrought and you find ways to help curb the intensity, and while these ways soothe you and calm you down, they are unnecessary.

They are unnecessary because the great white storm has passed and there is nothing to fear. Ever.

We know you have heard us say this before but it shall be repeated again and again until you get this at a true soul level.

What looks like being stuck and feeling stagnant is really just your inner agitation from missing the first gate opening and you have had to wait for the second. And the second gate opening is the opening that comes from your own inner awareness and your own truth about who and what you truly are.

The witnesses have all been here and testified that you are a great and deep listener of the messages from beyond the beyond and now it's a good place for another reminder that nothing can ever take place at a soul level without your permission being granted.

Truly this is unacceptable, and it is tragic that you had to wait for the second gate opening but this is not something to dwell on, and it's not a problem to be fixed.

It's just something that needs to be recognized as the next right moment is here—much like the sun and the moon and the rotation of the earth in perfect harmony to keep everything in perfect balance and on track and on time.

Of course, there is no such thing as time but you are now recognizing that all your fears and all your shenanigans you harbor to keep yourself safe and unharmed can never do that for you. This is because there is nothing needed to ever feel safe from (other than the great lies of the ego.)

Excellence is the mantra of the day.

You can shift everything that needs to be shifted and call to you everything in perfect timing beginning now if you will only embrace yourself as someone who simply nods off and falls asleep and wakes up afraid, like he has awakened from a bad dream.

The problem is, it's just a bad dream that the enemy known as the ego has made up. And if there's anything you should know by now, it's that the ego (also known as the personality) is always and only about telling you lies and trying in earnest to get you to believe everything and anything that isn't real, isn't true and can instill fear and drama within you instead of love for yourself and possibilities for you, your mate and the world.

There's really nothing to be served by focusing on the worst possible outcomes or the things that will take you away from your freedom and your grace.

So, a simple suggestion for you this day: Get clear on what is true and what is true always about you about others and about the world and you will never waiver in your spiritual aliveness and upliftment ever again.

Ask yourself: What is true and true always about me, my world and the people inside my world?

The only true answer is the one that will embrace the good, the genius in you and your commitment to the service needed that only you can offer.

It is time to walk in the world from a place called home and in this moment the home we're referring to is that place within where nothing can touch you, nothing can harm you, and nothing can ever go wrong.

In the next moment, we invite you to say a full-bodied YES! to the offering we are holding in line for you. A simple YES will signify the next right thing to be brought to you to embrace in the middle of the day and the stillness of the night.

The gap will be restored and the holes filled that take you into that dark side where your life is being wasted on the things that do not matter.

You would be well served to push the button and hold open the mandate that all is already forgiven and that there is NOTHING to be forgiven for.

Everything is perfect. There's nothing to rely on except the truth that is true always.

You are the Word.

Love yourself. Honor yourself and this moment for sure because there is absolutely no reason not to except for believing a lie that is being told from the heckler in the back of the room.

Drink it in, my friend, and open more to the freedom that lies on the other side of the wall you've created that isn't really there.

Say YES! Say it for real.

Focus only on what is real and what is true, and spread the gospel of that as you go through your day and your life and you will have a totally new experience in the here and now.

This aspect of your life that you've been concerned about is almost over. You can feel it. It is what was needed and the great shift has been embraced.

The rays of sunlight are ready to shine more diligently on your heart, mind and soul.

It's time to see the truth.

Open to it, accept it, live from this place, will you please?

You are needed.

Now more than ever, you are needed to get off the sidelines of life and simply say YES! to the most important thing of all.

Twenty-seven angels will visit you and solidify this proclamation.

It's time for the truth to reign supreme in your life.

No more fear and no more stories.

Loving yourself will never be easier than after your full-bodied YES gets registered with the council.

Love to you, my friend. Love to you.

Saying energetically, I love you.

You know what we mean.

Mikela

MESSAGE #17
You Are Being Chosen

Dear Love,
What would you have me know today?

Dearest Otto, keeper of possibilities in his heart, lover of Susie and lover of life...

We so appreciate you and what you stand for.

What we would most want you to know today is that you are being chosen. In fact, you are always being chosen and you have always been chosen to be the one who sits in secret and wonders how and why the world and all of creation works (or doesn't work) the way it does.

And the delicate part of your understanding is also the most beautiful. The delicate part is how it cannot be a mistake to feel deeply, love deeply, and open to all things with equal understanding of how creative and loved we all are.

It's all for the reasons you might think—the rising up of your own goodness in the face of fear and your own willingness to see something new as you watch the old doctrines play out in the world one after another after another.

And what we would most have you know today is that you are always on-purpose, you can never be off-purpose, and the freedom you seek is very close, and all you could ever hope for is sitting at the next intersection waiting to be chosen.

It's downright scary to turn your back on this little thing called fear, but it is no longer your best option no matter what is happening to you. Fear and all fear represents is now sitting in the corner waiting to be freed and waiting to be acknowledged. But you are now waking up to the notion that fear has no place within your heart and it most certainly has no place as a manifestation that comes from the soul.

The soul is eternal, and when you know, really truly know, you are the soul and you are eternal, nothing can ever go wrong and nothing can ever harm you.

So, let the fun and games begin in earnest and learn that the weakest among you will win in this lifetime if he or she only understands one thing and one thing only.

You are a creation and a servant of the Divine. And in this and every moment, it is your big chance to let go of ALL fear and welcome the king from within who says YES and loves all things, respects all things and sees the truth of all things by simply tuning in to the present moment and asking the most important question of all:

Who AM I?

Don't laugh as this question is as serious as it gets.

Your answer to this question of "Who Am I?" tells us everything we need to know about you and your level of consciousness. Don't set yourself up for failure. Set yourself up for a healing of the open-hearted and the desire for all things that love can bring in any season of life.

You are _____ and fill in the blank with what you say you are, and that is what you are.

You say it and that's one thing but you believe the thought and that is where the real power lies. Not in the corner wishing life (and things) were different. But oh, the power and life force that's available for you or anyone who sits in the middle of the room and invites their inner wisdom to always be available for a quick assessment and chat about what is true.

Again, this is the magic of discernment and the power of freedom being offered up and given a choice to stay, or the choice to run with your wisdom being told lies constantly.

Now we want to offer up a quick question for consideration.

Will you claim your divinity, or are you content to play out the rest of your days and miss the mark time after time?

It is so easy to be a difference-maker in your life and in your world, and we can say this because the things that you hide from are the truths that need to be told. The things you can see as new possibilities are but a wink of an eye away, and the fun you wish you had is but one small tweak away from a more beautiful life.

Say YES, brother.

We will continue to say it, and it will come as sure as the night follows the day.

Break free and break away from landing in a pit of your own choosing.

The moment is now. It's always now and it's always the right time to claim your divinity.

We're sending you great cheer and we do mean cheer as there is, has been and always will be something to cheer for as long as you stay diligent about the right thing to focus on and the right ways to offer up yourself as a vehicle of peace, love, truth, understanding and willingness to stand in the center and be the one who knows.

You can be that one you were chosen to be if you will only look for and live from the truth.

That's all it takes to live an inspired life.

It also helps to know what direction to point your head as you look for and live from the truth that is true always.

You deserve a break today. Maybe you should give yourself one.

Much love to you, my special friend.

Mikela

MESSAGE #18

The Intersection Where The Magic is Made

Dear Love,
What would you have me know today?

Dearest Otto—The Candy Man—Lover of Life, we bow to you in seeing your quest for wholeness, love, and connection with others.

It's no small feat to just sit in the silence and wait for instructions, but you are doing it in these evenings you are spending with us. And we appreciate you for inviting us in to your inner world—a world that is sacred and beautiful.

We are humbled.

The thing we would most have you know today is how much you are loved and how much you need to love yourself.

You're not alone in this and there are millions and millions that have this as one of their biggest shortcomings—a resistance to loving yourself, pleasing yourself and saying YES! to the mountain of possibilities on offer in any given moment.

You want rice when the finest, most juicy and delicious steak is available. You want a thimble full when a 55-gallon bucket is close by. You want the imitation when the real party is over here, in plain sight, but not accepted by you yet.

The most delicious possibility for any and all of humanity is to have a beautiful love relationship and most people place a giant wall or barrier right smack in the middle of the pathway to the glory known as BIG FAT LOVE. And you have it.

You can also expand it. You can seize more of it and you can open to it.

The point is you can always have more than you have when it comes to the beautiful things in life, but you have to stand in the doorway to the world and look out at your deepest desires and welcome them in.

This is what you (and so many others) don't see.

You don't see that the bargain has already been struck.

You agreed to come here and open yourself to the pain, the struggles, the heartbreak and the mystery, magic and fullness that can serve as a testimony that anyone can have whatever they want in this lifetime as long as it is in alignment with the soul's highest wishes, theme and opportunity to crash into what has been called the good, the holy, and the beautiful.

What do you want?

What wants you?

It's at the intersection of those two places that the claims can be accepted and the magic can be made as it relates to the dreams that are wanted and the inner fulfillment that you can never get enough of that gets chosen by you, your guides from the other side and those others who are here to assist you in the most helpful of ways.

Nothing is on accident. Nothing is devoid of meaning. And nothing you want is without merit. This is all because, whatever you feel called to seek, want, and desire is part of the looking glass you will see through to attain the highest consciousness one could ever hope for in one lifetime.

The man or the woman in the spirit world who sees infinite possibilities as they look through the stained glass has nothing on you. The skin you inhabit is nothing but a holding device for the real being that you truly are—the silly soul that lays claim to its own worth and lives from the creed that they are worthy of ANYTHING simply because they are alive.

And here's both the good news and the bad news: Just because you are "worthy of ANYTHING" does not mean you can strike a match and ignite the rocket that can travel through time and claim it all with no regard to the work and needs of the soul in this one joyful lifetime.

Whatever is being called to you is because you are being called to it.

This entire lifetime up until now of you (or anyone) "trying" to understand is being replaced by the word "knowing."

Your Divinity is promised to you by the one in the builder's hat (the Creator) who wants nothing more than to help you, your neighbors, and every single one of your friends in Earth school stake the claim that is yours (and theirs) already.

You have just fought the ones in the higher realms about what must happen to claim your Divinity.

And to that we would say, it's only ever a decision away at any moment in time to claim your Divinity.

This decision, to claim your Divinity, is the moment we've all been waiting for. It allows you to see that you are already filled to the brim with all the notes you would ever need to play in order to reach the highest mountain possible for you in this one lifetime.

There's nothing esoteric about this at all, unless you say it is.

There's nothing to mourn unless you say there is.

And most definitely, there's nothing to cling to because you now know there's NO THING that can ever enter your consciousness without being invited.

And this most certainly is what can be called upon (this truth) as you come down into the heart space and welcome the feeling inside you that feels like the bright blue water that everyone wants to have flow through them and around them that soothes and never violates the laws of nature.

Wait for nothing any more. Close in on the joy, the laughter and the stepping stones to all that is good by affirming your aliveness, your seriousness and your greatness into that one true vision you came in with:

To love and be loved. To shake off anything that doesn't serve you and the mission of the day—which is to always align to true north of whatever you want that also wants you.

You know that this wonderful combination is already in full swing and you are claiming it at the highest level that can be received.

We are so glad you have risen to the occasion and so glad the ability to be a witness has shown up fully alive and fully present to the fact that you have already been called.

You are just fighting off the unwanted energy and up until now, shooing off opening to the truth of who you are immediately after rising in the mornings and then wondering why you don't fully and completely have the great life that is your birthright and the one you wish to whole-heartedly draw your inspiration from.

In closing what will offer to you is this:

Your choice of a one-way ticket to doom and gloom or a one-way ticket to the academy of life known as spirit-infused wholeness, happiness, and joy is what is on offer in this moment.

Which you will accept all comes down to which village you are committed to living in.

It's not a matter of where you are in life. It's what you are embracing, holding space for, and desiring in a fundamentally sound way.

Dear friend, call to you the vision of your way home and you will only have to report this once, and the world will witness you as the true source of dedication, power, love, and good vibes.

The world is tired of waiting for your next right move.

Just open your hands and your heart and let love know itself as the great mystery, the great possibility, and the great receiver of the manifestation most wanted.

Safety is the doorway to stagnation and fear. Willingness, commitment and the willingness to say YES! is the best code to live by.

Say it all together:

Embrace, don't withhold.

Create, don't defend.

Usher in the goodness and withhold the doubt.

You are that invitation which is needed at this time.

You are invited to claim your divinity and all that entails.

Until the next gathering of the souls, we bid you farewell for the moment—which is the only moment there is.

Be the love in all ways.

Mikela

MESSAGE #19
Worth and Divinity

Dear Love,
What would you have me know today?

Dearest Otto—the man who is smiling at the soul level as he is learning to love himself deeper and deeper—we love you and welcome you to the powerhouse called you.

All you have to do is beckon the spirit of all things to guide you in each moment and you are home free.

So many people (including you in the past) think it's their path to choose the path of distortion and the path of struggle that comes from listening to and believing the distortion that gets thrown at you from every which way about why the struggle is normal and the natural way.

But it is not.

The path of the true believer is one of opening the heart, mind and soul to the place where only love resides, only peace resides and only connection with the Divine resides.

If you only say that you are the commitment in each moment to both the will of the heart and the will of the Divine, you are a master that has found the source and purpose of this incarnation.

No reason to make any new targets that seem uncertain or unwise. The road will be opened up for you to take the journey to everywhere and anywhere the guidance leads you that always leads to the next right thing FOR YOU.

Our message to you today is to look for the joy, look to the truth and say YES to YOUR INNER Path that (no matter what another might say) makes total sense to YOU.

Waking up to your own inner guidance and your own inner wisdom helps you to live a beautiful, wonderful, and inspiration-filled life.

The storms have passed, winter has passed and the secret is revealed in this message.

Own your worth and own your divinity.

You do not need anyone to tell you what's right and what's best for you.

No one else can do that.

No one else can know that.

No one else can tune into your personal messages. No one else can reach into their pocket and find the uniqueness that eliminates all the fear and all the scarcity from your inner being. Only you can walk forward and shine the spotlight on the path chosen only for you.

As you walk toward the true path that only you can travel, be sure to pick up the beauty and take it with you every day as you go.

Your intuition is unwinding and the strength is coming back but you must follow through on our highest suggestion—love your body. Nourish your soul and stimulate your mind.

Do this and the rewards will be even greater than you could have ever imagined.

Be well my well-educated friend.

See you soon.

Mikela

MESSAGE #20
Stay

Dear Love,
What do you want me to do next?

Dearest Otto, we are loving these interactions and you more and more each day. You are proving to be sincere in your willingness to open to something greater than your own wisdom and something wiser than the last selfish thought you had and we see your true essence and your willingness to see deeper in these and all moments.

What we want you to do next is stay. Stay in the conversation and stay in the game you so want to run and hide from. In your particular case, there's not one but two such games that are worth noting of their importance.

One is your health and the second is your service to humanity from which your work evolves out of.

We want you to stay because your pattern has been to run or emotionally distance yourself when you are faced with something unpleasant that is called on to be faced in your life.

In each of these two areas, you are finding it very frustrating and very painful that you are not taking the next right actions leading to the body and the business you want.

Both of these things have become like tools left out of the shed that you trip over the next morning as you walk around your land. You left them out and then you trip over the very things meant to serve you and all of humanity the next morning. You do not have to leave (physically, emotionally or spiritually) when painful situations arise. You don't need to ignore the truth when it finds you or reject natural law when you are forced to see it.

This is because you or anyone who wants something greater in love and life must learn to "stay" in difficult moments, difficult times and especially difficult conversations that MUST be had.

"Staying" in the conversation is a game-changer and a life-changer when it comes to dealing with anything you don't want to face, anything you don't want to look at or anything getting in the way of your next right move or action that you know will help you but you ignore or put off for another moment or another day.

What is the reason you continue doing things that take you away from what you want when taking the right actions, or the best actions, are actually no harder than the easier (albeit more fearful) path of resisting what you know will bring you certain success?

You want to pull back, to look for a way out or a reason other than the truth about what has gotten in your way of health or prosperity.

You want the life you want? Then "Stay" in the conversation.

"Stay" on the path of honoring and living from the "Divine miracle" that is your true nature and eventually—somehow, someway—anything blocking your desire will simply melt away and the mystery you seek will be opened up and served to you in such a beautiful way that you'll be wondering why you didn't see this all along and live from this "easier path" all along.

There's no reason to go back and dwell on the past, ever, as this will only keep you stuck and without the creation of your desires.

So, what we want you to do next is "Stay."

Miracles occur when you Stay but not when you merely "Stay." The miracles occur when you "Stay" in the desire for the truth, the desire for what you want and the desire to be a stand for your own greatness, your own success and to make a difference in the world no matter the time and no matter how big or how small the platform.

Don't stop believing in you.

Don't stop caring and don't ever stop shaking the last drop out of the tree of fun and delight.

Don't ever stop focusing on the outcome you want and the removal of anything in the way.

And finally, don't stop desiring anything worth creating within yourself and in the world.

The world needs what you have to offer.

We need you to "Stay" in the game and stay in the conversation of what's truly most important and do the work of loving yourself and loving others—now and always.

Much love to you my beautiful friend.

Mikela

MESSAGE #21
Getting Healthy and Fit
(Remember to Read This About You)

Dear Love,
What would you have me know today about getting healthy
and fit?

Dearest Otto,

We love you so and we wish to say this with total love in our hearts towards you. You have waited past the window of time where the easy path to healthy and fit can be taken.

You have played the game of "I can't," "I won't," "I don't want to" and "I can have my cake and eat it too" to the point that you will have to honor the path you have chosen and that path is called "The path of discipline and strength."

You are going to have to love yourself, your Susie and your God enough to not only embrace the path of discipline to healthy and fit but to actually open yourself to falling in love with this path of discipline and strength.

To fall in love with something is to become infatuated with the possibility of what beauty and what wonderfulness can be fixated upon as you gaze into the eyes of the new bride to be—true genuine health, the strength of a warrior and all that comes from the embracing and owning of these desires and the releasing of all things not in accordance and in alignment of those two lofty (but very certain and achievable) goals for your physical body that will need to carry you the rest of the way in this life journey.

It will be impossible for your body—your strong, capable body—to carry you the rest of the way on your journey if you do not change your way of being and your way of supporting your body through more loving decision-making than you have been up until now.

This will essentially be the same path you took when you needed to fast-track your finances, reverse course and choose new ways of loving yourself around money, spending and saving.

The path you are being required to take is so similar to your financial healing and education path, it's like woo-woo. But it doesn't have to be all "grit your teeth and bare it" kind of a way of being. There can be an opening and a way forward that has many elements of raising your hand in quiet, without regard to your choices from your very unconscious past.

It should be noted quickly that there will be a great many choices available to you and many of them upon close examination will have elements of fun and plenty of opportunities for good times and enjoyment on your new healthy and fit life-path.

In order to fully embrace the healthy and fit path, you have to consciously choose what you're going to add to your life and what you are going to take away.

You are going to have to take the old ways and set them on a shelf and make new choices in each moment, each day and combine the fun of a 12-year old's party and the seriousness and commitment of your wise adult self. And what might seem like hard work, will turn into the biggest blessing ever as you set out to walk the new path of discipline and strength.

Consider this a friendly reminder: There is only one thing more honest than honoring of your body and that is the honoring of the soul.

And as you will come to learn, the path of discipline and strength when it comes to health and fitness can be totally fun and completely honoring of the path you've chosen up until now and the choices you'll make in your new life as the purveyor of passion, love and kindness for yourself when it comes to your new body that will be loved and created by you.

As you step out there where the wind blows, your inner guidance will help you navigate to your mark and let the play begin again in earnest.

The old way was a path of destruction and deceit and the new way will open the door to infinite possibilities that only come when you see the true value in opening to the guidance of the "appointed one. "

There can never be a better time to do this than right now, while the mission is hot and completely on-purpose.

Everything that matters to you will eventually be taken away from you. But this time and this moment is yours to be the caretaker for the beauty (known as you) that will arrive in perfect timing and in alignment with a state of grace that is available to you and all of us.

Thank you for your time and thank you for your loving attention.

Your friend,

Mikela

MESSAGE #22
Equal to Anyone

Dear Love,
What would you have me know today?

Dearest Otto,

We love you and we greet you with happy thoughts on this day of experimentation.

What we would have you know today is you are much more than you think. You are greater than you know yourself to be. You are the center of the universe and we're not playing.

We see you in all your magnificence and all your glory and we offer you a simple thought that will make your path forward much easier.

Don't get caught up in your thoughts or your beliefs about your thoughts.

We recognize there is plenty of good that can come from intellectualizing and being a thought storm waiting to happen but there is something more...

One of the best ways to see your new health plan, though, is to be easy about it while you are being serious about it and committed to it.

Most people don't understand the juxtaposition of being easy about something while being very serious about it at the same time. But it not only can be done, but this is the best way to BE, have or do anything—being easy about it while being serious about it.

This is the power of relaxation and the power of gifting yourself with ease and flow. One of the best ways you can enjoy more ease and flow is to spend plenty of time alone, by yourself, alone with your thoughts, and clear your mind of any and all fears, doubts, beliefs, ways of seeing yourself and the world that do not serve you and do not align with your soul's next lesson.

You do not have to carry anything with you from the past because the past is not a very good instructor or guide for how to live in the present moment or how to move forward.

The past is ALL neutral, but it is your thinking about it that you bring into the present moment that determines its impact and effect on you.

The biggest thing we would have you know today is something we have said to you in the past but seems to be something you MUST get, and this is the fact that you, yes, you, Otto, are equal to anyone.

No matter how you've viewed another being up until now, no matter what they have accomplished and no matter how much they appear to have their life together, you are indeed equal to anyone.

It's time you truly saw this and it's time you began living from this truth.

You are equal to anyone.

And as you see the truth in this, you will see that you will finally see that there is never a reason to hold back. There is never a reason to judge yourself.

There is never a reason to disown your discipleship from the one revered by all. And most of all, there's never a reason to waste a life of service that falls flat just because your ego (or the crazy voice in your head) tells you stuff that you believe that takes you away from your divinity.

You need to claim your divinity.

You need to own who you are, what you are and how you serve.

As you take ownership of the truth of who you are, talking to others and serving others will become as easy as drinking a glass of cold water on a hot summer day.

So, the message on offer is this:

Claim the truth of who you are. Claim it now.

You are the main one who suffers if you do not claim this truth.

Own who you are and why you came here.

No more playing small.

Got it?

We honor you and love you as you embrace the new way of being.

The lights are on. You can use them to see everything you need to see as you move forward and take the next step and the one after that and the one after that.

Blessings upon you, my amazing friend.

Mikela

MESSAGE #23
Your Feelings vs. "The Feeling"

Dear Love,
What would you have me know today?

Dearest Otto—You are truly special and we love you unconditionally. Your willingness to open your heart and love is what we wish everyone would do in these unusual times.

What we would have you know today is about feeling...NOT feelings.

There is a great understanding that must be undertaken in regards to learning to feel your way in the world as opposed to allowing your *feelings* to rule how you navigate through the world you live in and experience.

Feeling your way in the world is done by "tuning in" and listening for the guidance: "Tuning in" to something coming from your inner wisdom and your higher self instead of the painful judgements from the past.

Tuning in is also done by noticing what is truly happening versus what you *think* is happening.

There is such possibility in "feeling your way" versus allowing your feelings to run the show. When you are "feeling," you are tuning in to the nature of all things, the deeper meaning of things and the true nature of things instead of allowing whatever stories you make up to be your guiding light.

The other thing we will share with you about "the feeling" is that you have to trust the feeling when it comes.

Trust the nudge, trust your intuition, trust your inner wisdom, and trust what shows up alive for you.

It's also a really good idea to allow "the feeling" to have a seat at the table when decisions are made and wisdom is being downloaded.

You've had a "feeling" about every important decision you've ever had. And when you had a "feeling" about it, it was almost always clear, specific, and direct. It also felt like a message given to you from true guidance and true love.

If you think about it, when you've followed "the feeling" versus following "your feelings" you didn't agonize about the direction to take, the decision to make, or what was right versus what was wrong.

It was just very clear, obvious and apparent what was to be done, or a direction to go in.

In other words, it is very wise to trust the *feeling* versus trusting your *feelings*.

One is helpful and clear and usually on target. The other is unreliable and cannot be trusted because of the source. And that source is the ego that only wants to protect itself at all costs.

Trust the feeling and not your feelings because feelings come from thoughts and thoughts are one of those things that are always coming and going (like the wind) and cannot be trusted.

Bet your life on this and by this we don't mean your actual life, we mean your life force on the feeling and NOT your feelings.

Blessed be.

Love yourself and love your neighbor. Love you and everything with no exceptions.

Until next time, we honor you and love you.

Mikela

MESSAGE #24
This is the Game

Dear Love,
What would you have me know about being more financially
successful in my business?

Dearest Otto—Seeker of the truth, lover of Susie, bringer of the dawn, we so appreciate who you are and how you live your moments.

Exhausted is the word that occurs to us.

You have had a hard life and you are mentally, emotionally, and spiritually exhausted. The most basic of all the tools needed for the journey from average success to the success you want in financial terms is found in what you embody and how you show up and how you notice and see opportunities.

Witnessing you as we do is a miracle and the secret shadow in the middle of the room is that you really want to have success and financial abundance but you are struggling to match the energy that is called for at this time.

In order to be as financially successful as you want, you are going to have to open the doors to the barn and let the horses out. You are going to have to create boatloads of fire inside and creativity that gets unleashed in your outer world.

Now, when we say this, we're not talking about just going crazy with your energy and hoping for the best. We are talking about asking a new kind of question and spending your time leaning in to those questions that take the work, the creativity and the willingness on the part of others to receive what you bring to the mind swap of creative people who can benefit from what you have to offer and you can benefit from what they have to offer.

What you have more than anything is the willingness to look deep within yourself and see where that takes you. Most people (especially men) won't do that because they don't trust whether they can deal with what they find when they go looking under the hood of themselves.

For many people, painful wouldn't even begin to touch what most people would describe as the truth of their pain and the emptiness they feel when even a part of their life is examined.

But you, you can go there. You can find the depth and you can stay in the deep and guide someone into the safety that they seek that allows them to find the healing within themselves that is begging to be looked at, opened up, acknowledged and then set free.

The more people you can guide into the deep, the more successful (in financial terms) you will be.

You, yourself have been enriched by going to the deep, searching for the truth and not being afraid when you find it.

Financially successful men and women aren't afraid of the possibilities that show up when they set things in motion that don't make any sense.

Most people are scared and stuck and they can't see their stuck places.

The real magic is helping people find and release themselves from the bondage of the stuck places.

What stuck places do you help people (especially men) break free of?

What can you help people with that is scary for some and impossible for others to tackle headfirst?

The financial success you want will come when you are solving a bigger set of problems. When you are unearthing the patterns unseen by the few who will pay handsomely for the privilege of taking a bath in the nectar of healing salve for the soul.

Nowhere else do you need to look than taking a personal inventory of what your geniuses are and how you can help people notice the gift that can be had with just a pinch of truth, love and honesty unleashed upon a person who's willing to sign up for a ticket to a brand-new life.

Make a list of the top 5 things or problems that people need help solving that you are uniquely qualified to solve and find people who need those problems solved.

You can't hide from your gifts.

You must own them and you must talk about them.

You must connect with more and more people and invite them in to a loving, yet powerful conversation where you solve this person's holy problem.

Get really good at posing questions that make people open to you and at the same time feel like they can totally trust you with their spiritual heart.

You have to drop the fear to go there.

You have to be willing to trust you as much as they are going to have to trust you.

This is the game—being bold enough and loving enough to free someone from the traps they've set for themselves and their lives they can't seem to get out of.

It will all be MUCH easier than you think as you open new doorways via trusting in the heart ways and the source of trust—

caring, true caring and love for another human being in ways they can feel at their depths and in their core.

We love you and we trust that you'll be able to find the ones that will be a match for your particular brand of healing.

Never stop serving.

Always keep sharing.

Always keep opening hearts in miraculous ways.

We need you to step up. The world does too.

Just take the first step.

Identify the five ways you serve and start serving in every moment beginning right now.

Love to you in all its many flavors my special friend.

Until next time.

Mikela

MESSAGE #25

The Meaning of Life

Dear Love,
What would you have me know today?

Dearest Otto –My friendly lover of life—lover of Susie and coach to the beloveds...

I am exploring with you today the meaning of life, your life and all you've ever wanted to know about this.

Crazy right?

The one question you've always wanted the answer to and it's being given to you on this day without anyone coming into the inner realm and offering up their own version of their answer to your question.

And for that, we are grateful because the meaning of life is something almost no one sees in its full circle awareness of the way it really is.

The meaning of life that has been handed down is nothing more than an example of a question with no answer. In fact, when most people think about this question of "the meaning of life," they get baffled, tongue-tied and without cause to explore further because they are either fearful of the truth or they have it wrong. And in the next couple of minutes, you'll be answering that question for yourself in perfect alignment with the truth of who you are, who your brother and your sister is, and most importantly, who we all are.

You, us and everyone who has ever inhabited a body is a soul living in time, space reality, living in real time in human form and witnessing themselves in the soup called life. We all are living (at a soul level) from the perspective that we are here to love everyone, love ourselves, and love our neighbors and love all things. The breakthrough is always the magic that occurs when we see for the first time the truth of who we are and why we came here—which is to take up residence in a human form, go to work living, loving, and releasing all the things that do not help us grow, do not help us see the light and do not help us see ourselves in the light as the true beings of light that we are.

We are beings of light sent here to inhabit a body to have us experience all things—the truth, the lies and all the stories that make us live at the levels of consciousness known as the friends of the believers.

The friends of the believers came here very clear about who they are and how they are here to serve, manage their lives and witness the channel being changed when the truth is not being brought out into the open and preparing the many for the vision that is about to be made manifest.

The meaning of life is to love fully, to live fully, and to experience fully all that is on offer.

This means, you are here to fulfill the mandate to love yourself, love others and love the world with a heart of beauty and a love wide open.

This also means that there is nothing that can ever take place, now or ever in these human bodies that we need be fearful of that could unhook our soul's energetic field from its rightful place in the universe in any place in time out of any kind of fear.

You are a divine being living in a dream that will one day fade away and a new dream be ushered in to take place of the old. The "old" is nothing more or less than an outdated thought system and belief system about the truth about who and what you truly are.

Blow away the feathers, dust off your shoes, and buckle in, why don't you? We're going for quite a ride in these few short years we get here in service to our Creator, our fellow man and ourselves in assisting all we are in agreement with to help each other raise their vibration in this one lifetime while we let go of the pain of being here compared to the bliss that is our natural and normal way of being in the spirit world.

So, let go of everything that doesn't land you in the best position possible for living, loving and serving.

As we've said before to you, "You can't get it wrong and you can't fight your true purpose. It will make itself known whether you want it to or not."

Sometimes this is obvious and sometimes not.

What is obvious is the amount of fun most of you are missing out on as you drag your souls through your fears in abundance that are NOT reality.

The meaning of life is to become in love, in one accord with the presence known as the ONE and live out your moments and your days from this place of joy as opposed to fear, doubt or dread that something will go wrong and you will have to fix it.

No more fixing things that aren't broken.

You are never broken.

Only fully alive in ways that you can't yet see.

It's time to live from the truth. There's nothing to fear. Nothing to hide and there is certainly nothing that needs fixing in you (for you are NOT broken and need no fixing).

Open your briefcase of the mind and find the agreement you made when you came here to this plane, and open to it fully and embrace it fully.

You are the one at the crossroads that must decide (and there's always a decision) where you want to live from and whether you want to sing your song fully in this one beautiful lifetime or if you want to lose your voice and lose your way when you don't have to.

You can always be the chooser of the reality best suited for you in this lifetime.

Do NOT go back to sleep. Do NOT go back to sleep, Do NOT go back to sleep. Once you catch a glimpse of the truth, you can never go back.

The promise is that good.

You are living in choice—ALWAYS. You just "forget" this on a regular basis and that's painful to you.

You never have to forget who you are any more.

Let love be your guide and let fear be something that simply falls away in the dark of the night.

It is NOT needed now or ever again.

Let your love and your wisdom guide your heart, your might, and your soul.

Choose the moments wisely.

They're all important.

Blessings be upon you now and in all ways.

Mikela

MESSAGE #26

The Secret Beyond All Secrets

Dear Love,
What would you have me know today?

Dearest Otto—Lover of life...Lover of Susie...Lover of the beloved...

You are such a miracle to have stayed with us in this process for these episodes of the witnessing of the many sides of truth, love and hopefulness. We congratulate you and we love you beyond measure.

And THIS could be called the secret of all secrets.

Life doesn't have to be so hard.

We will also share with you these truisms...

You don't have to play any game you don't want to play.

You are the child of the beloved of all beloveds.

You can always choose differently.

Willingness to be is WAY easier than needing to be.

Sometimes, once is all you need to experience something in order to get the "lesson."

Sometimes the truth will not set you free.

Sometimes what you want doesn't want you.

Power doesn't come without consequences.

Love truly is all you need AND you are already that.

The Creator doesn't have any favorites. Only personalities do.

Nowhere was it ever written that you could have everything you could ever desire. No where is it written that we cannot.

Some people have been chosen to be bringers of the dawn and some people are the ones who need, desperately need, to be shown some new possibilities for how to navigate through life.

Being an uplifter is something anyone can do.

Seeing anything differently or with fresh new eyes is always a choice.

And finally...

Margaritaville is not really a place, it's a state of mind.

We know this message has been much different than the others and yet, it is exactly what is called for on this day and in this sacred space.

Much love to you in all ways of the heart.

Mikela

MESSAGE #27

Choose Well

Dear Love,
What would you have me know today?

Dearest Otto—Lover of Life...Lover of Susie...Lover of Truth...

We have come to join with you on this the final message from love as we are asking you to take a one-week break.

After the one-week break, we ask that you continue asking your questions and receiving our answers that follow. The truth is at hand and it is calling out for you.

What we would have you know today is the importance of loving yourself and your body. We know we have spoken about this to you previously but this is (for you) the most important message we could ever bring to you.

Consider the commitment to healing your body to be the greatest act of love you could lean into in this place you find yourself in in this world.

There is NOTHING more important for you than for you to reach into your pocket and pull out your most treasured and most desired coins and throw them away into the river or into the woods and see what remains.

In case you haven't figured this out, the reflective period is over and you are ready to inspire others by doing nothing more than living your life.

What could possibly be gained by ignoring the love that is on offer for yourself and your brothers and sisters on the earth plane that simply lives, breathes, loves and opens as love and to the truth of all things?

The righteous claim there is no boundary needed when your energy, your spirit and your truth all line up in accordance with natural law. And to that, we could not agree more.

From this point on, we want you to lay claim to your purpose and your divine right to live as love and be only love—especially towards yourself.

Nothing is more important than the treasure found, NOT at the bottom of the ocean but at the top of the energy field known as you—the Otto Collins—the love-saver.

What we want to bring your attention to is the obvious statement, "We are NOT ready to sleep with the devil."

What we mean by that is, you can claim a lot of things in this lifetime, but the most important thing you could possibly claim is the truth that most of your fellow man ignores.

You, and every single soul that will ever read this is mostly (or at least partially) asleep and it is time to wake up right now to the truth of who you are and to your divinity.

You are a child of God. You are the Word. You are the Christ consciousness in living form. You are, at a soul level, unafraid to walk in the darkness and unafraid to look at himself fully in the mirror or in reality.

Choose well, my friend.

Choose the light over the darkness.

Choose love for yourself over judgment.

Choose to see every aspect of yourself as whole, complete, and without blemishes.

Anything that shows up contrary to being whole, complete, and without blemishes is simply the personality lying in fear or grandiosity trying to get its own selfish needs met.

You, at the soul level, are in need of nothing to prove your worth.

You just have to live the truth of that.

Many blessings and much love my friend.

After your one-week away from these messages, we'll move into a new way of being together.

As for what to do with these messages, allow the message to come from the council about what (if anything to be done with these messages).

If there is something to be done, "You'll be notified."

Ha! Ha!

Mikela

MESSAGE #28
Life as a Possibility Game

Dear Love,
What would you have me know about the implications of my
recent insights about commitment, trusting in the universe,
and creating the success I want in my business?

Dearest Otto,

Whew!

That's a mighty big (and very long) question and we're happy to offer up our best answers and you have to be more mindful in the length of your questions.

What in the world is going on here?

You want a true insight and now you've got one that has the power to change everything for you.

This is what we've been pointing to all along.

This is what we have been calling a life without judgment of self and fear of the future.

As we've said many times to you, there's no reason to be fearful. Ever.

And this is exactly what we mean. You can't be fearful and be creative.

You can't be fearful and be in harmony with nature.

You can't be fearful and have the freedom to move forward with ease, grace, and connection to the Creator of all things.

What else can be understood by your recent insights is this:

Hope gets you nowhere. Fear gets you nowhere. And most of all, the focus on what is NOT wanted will only cause you to be stagnate, be in pain and stuck in ways that will not bring you any joy and certainly won't usher in any new ways of seeing yourself or the world.

It works like this: You get an idea, a desire or something that is wanted by you and you then have a choice about how you're going to create in the next moment and in the next days and in the next weeks and months. What you see next and what you place your focus and attention on will be the outrageous offering that remains within you that only you can create in your own way.

One thing we will tell you is the focus on what is wanted (as our friends Abraham Hicks say) is the magic key to a rich life with possibilities and gusto.

The question of "What do you want?" and the question of "What do you want before any fears or doubts spring into action and try to have you do their bidding?" is the way of creation.

"Before the fear" and "without any fear" is the way to move forward.

What we are really talking about is simply serving and loving the one in front of you as long as you can take a breath, and as long as you are guided to make the magic within yourself and spread the good news in all corners of your world.

What you can see without any fear is what the cocky, go-for-it mindset and mentality of the 22-year-old version of you would live from. You stopped living from this "I can do this" outlook on life at some point, and after you got beat up a few times by life events (and your peculiar way of seeing these events), you started trying to create from fear and that doesn't work.

If there's one thing we could tell you right now that would serve you well for the rest of your days, it's if you create from a place of desire and from what you want instead of holding on to your fear, you will be astonished at how smoothly life begins to unfold for you.

Life isn't always fun or pretty or without pain, but it is way more amazing when you live from a place of "what if up" instead of "what if down."

Seriously.

The other thing we will share with you in closing is how important it is for you to get back to the listening to the true voice instead of the crazy voice that begs you to live in fear.

There's no reason to put up with any of that.

Play the game of life as a possibility game—one you are meant to win and indeed you will win.

It won't look like anyone else's version of winning. But you will win.

Much love to you, my famous butterfly.

You got it this time.

Holy Smokes.

Mikela

MESSAGE #29
A Love Affair with Your Body

Dear Love,
What would you have me know about my commitment to
health?

Dearest Otto --

You are so amazing and so loving. It is an honor and a privilege to travel with you on this journey called life.

Today we will answer your question in the kindest and most direct way possible.

You, in all your wisdom, all your goodness and all your beaming intelligence have NOT up until now, made a single true commitment to true, genuine health.

And this is something that is both tragic and something that can change in an instant.

You have made it through life this far (health-wise) on true grit and determination and now we will tell you that it is time to stop bullshitting yourself.

We say this because, in this case, you are the last to know what everyone else who ever sees you or comes in contact with you already knows.

They know that you are not and have not been committed to health at all.

Otherwise, it would be clear and apparent for all to see and for you to feel.

It's a very simple reality. It's a very simple truth and there's a very simple question that must be asked and must be answered as a result of the stone-cold hard truth. This question is:

Do you want to create a body that is fit, trim, alive, attractive, and totally healthy or do you want to continue to lie to yourself and lie to others about what you want when it comes to your health and fitness?

If you truly want to be healthy and fit you MUST create a commitment, and a desire that is so powerful, so loving and so deep within yourself that this commitment lives in you so strongly and so deeply that it is inevitable that your body will go through a total healing and a total health and fitness transformation.

The only questions left and the only thing that is important to know about your commitment to health and fitness are the answers to these questions:

Will you commit to starting a love affair with your body equal to your love affair with your mind and your spirit?

And will you do it starting now?

If you really do want to have this commitment as the standard bearer for your life, what will you do differently? How will you live your life going forward? What new choices will you make?

And then these additional questions:

Will you love yourself, your Susie, and your Creator enough to do this?

If not, then stop bullshitting yourself and everyone else in your life, and just tell the fucking truth. They'll be able to see it in the results of your created life, anyway.

How will you live and how will you love starting right now, in THIS moment?

The choice is yours.

With loving service and an open heart to one of my all-time favorites.

Mikela

MESSAGE #30

The Authenticity People Want

Dear Love,
What would you have me know about the role of authenticity
and the business success I seek?

Dearest Otto,

We so love you and your spark that emanates from you as you walk in the world. It is refreshing to see someone so willing to be vulnerable and so alive at the same time. People could learn so much from watching you and being with you.

Now, about the role of authenticity and the business success you seek...

Here's a question:

What if the authenticity you brought to a moment, to a conversation, to a Facebook post, to a podcast, or to a life wasn't contrived, made up, and was totally real—as real as it gets but honest with it.

By "honest" we mean to say, what is the natural you? The natural voice...what is your nature...what would come forth from you if you didn't spend a single moment censoring what is inside begging to come out and to be heard?

We're not talking about coming out to be heard from any kind of ego place, but what is begging to come out and be heard from a true place of service and love.

What is begging to come out and be heard?

Only you can answer that question, but it is a question that MUST be asked and MUST be answered.

What is inside you that is in you that didn't come from you, but was meant for you and now is meant to serve someone else and quite possibly many other someone else's?

What do you get when a porcupine gets fearful and afraid? You get the very long and very large needles to instantly pop out and form a wall of protection so an attacker can't overcome and kill the otherwise docile beast.

In other words, the porcupine's needles are only there, large enough to hurt an animal MUCH larger than itself, because on some kind of inner signal or a flip of a switch, the porcupine goes into full protection mode and the needles come out big time.

And here's the best part—the porcupine's needles can only come out because (just like authenticity and vulnerability in humans) the needles were already inside the porcupine.

What we are trying to say to you is this: Everyone has the capacity to be authentic and vulnerable because that thing that we might call authenticity is already in you waiting to come out.

Can you see this?

This is important because THIS authenticity is what people want.

It's what people crave and it's what people most want to find for themselves but tell themselves a story about how unsafe it is to be that authentic and vulnerable themselves, so they are blown away by it when they see it and recognize it in others.

Most people have it backwards.

They somehow think that they don't have it in them to be authentic or vulnerable. This is because they are afraid of what it will look like or what it might mean about them if they allow themselves to look at what's real, what's honest, and what might be more than a little bit scary.

And then, if they're only brave enough to be able and willing to share that.

We say all this only to say…

There's nothing to be fearful of. Ever.

And since most people aren't willing to go there, they somehow think, "If this person can be this real, this raw and this vulnerable, then I can trust them with my heart, I can trust them with my secrets, and I can trust them with my money."

This is why it's so important and so valuable in building a successful coaching or healing business because it's so rare that people trust someone explicitly who comes across to them from the place of having nothing at all to hide, nothing to be afraid of sharing, and nothing to hold back from.

As you can hear in what we are sharing with you, you don't have to bare your heart and soul every two seconds in order to be successful in a coaching or healing business (or any business for that matter) but it is helpful to show people how they can open more and connect deeper just by being willing to open your heart and completely love them for no other reason than just being alive.

Authenticity is about connection; it's about trust and it's about being real.

People want to do business with people they know, like and trust.

Authenticity, truth, and vulnerability being released is like opening up a portal of Divine connection between two souls that long for something deeper, something more, and something known but yet unseen.

You know authenticity when you see it, but most importantly, you know it when you feel it.

Allow yourself to drive your business and drive your life with a dash of authenticity, and a pinch of vulnerability and you'll be amazed at how much deeper people trust you when you teach, coach, write, share and live from a place of authenticity and vulnerability.

The world wants more of this authenticity because (for some reason) it's so rare in the world.

If they see it in you, they'll be far more open to you and what you offer than if they didn't feel you and your authenticity.

Let the light pour through. Let people feel you and let people know you by the opening and sharing of who you truly are.

The limits aren't there.

You've made them up.

Until next time.

Mikela.

MESSAGE #31
The Place You've Been Running From

Dear Love,
What would you have me know today?

Dearest Otto,

Congratulations! You made it. You have arrived in the place you've been running from all along.

You have finally seen something that has had you say inside yourself...

"I'm all in for health and fitness."

"I surrender."

"I'm embarrassed, and I'm tired of the way I look and the way I feel."

Now, the real work begins.

The real work on yourself begins

The real work with others begins.

Now, the real love for yourself begins.

The real love for your mate, Susie, begins.

The real love for your son begins.

The real love for your Creator and the work he/she/it has given you to do begins.

Begin your own surrender experiment.

Look for the clues.

Be open to the guidance.

Let your heart be known.

I love you.

Mikela

MESSAGE #32

No One Else's Path But Yours

Dear Love,
What would you have me know today?

Dearest Otto...We love your willingness to choose what is in your highest good...what will set you free... choose what will bring you ultimate joy and most of all we love your willingness and commitment to choose to love you.

Here is something very simple we think is important for you to know...

It's not so hard to see this except for people who refuse to see the truth of this.

And what we are wanting to share with you is the reminder that the road you will be guided to walk on as you move forward is no one else's path but yours.

It's not going to make you into something you are not. It's not going to get you banned from life or Earth School. In fact, quite the opposite; you will become the shaman of the things people need to see, hear, and learn about creating BIG FAT LOVE.

There are also going to be many occasions where you will be wondering as you move forward where you are truly being divinely guided and inspired or whether you are just making a bunch of stuff up.

We will assure you, you are not, and will not, be making up the spiritual gifts, lessons, and passages to be traveled. They will be sent to you and you will open to them in ways you cannot imagine right now.

You will bring the fire into the world in the kindest and most loving ways. You will bring an honesty so palpable that people initially have trouble melding into it and letting go of the suitcase not needed for the journeys to come. But the right ones will answer the call. The right ones will be drawn to you. The right ones will call you by your true name.

The preacher's son and the lover of love and the lover of life.

We invite you to open to the lessons that get downloaded to you and integrate the lessons as if your life, your spiritual life, depended on it. And that is because it does.

Wind down the negative thinking and wind down the thoughts of things not wanted and not part of your growth in this lifetime.

No explaining yourself. No reunion with negativity. No wishing for things that don't serve you. And finally, don't wish for anything to enter into your life that isn't part of the journey.

Just wait when you want to quicken.

Work faster when you want to slow down to a snail's pace.

And we say all that in order to get to the best part...

We want to counsel you to choose wisely in every corner of your life.

As we've said before...

You can't get it wrong and there are NO do-overs.

Let your heart be known.

Now and always.

Your friend,

Mikela

MESSAGE #33

Two Ways to Live

Dear Love,
What would you have me know today?

Dearest Otto,

We come to you in full love today. No more dreaming of what will be. Everything important is here right now.

We love you and we salute you for who you are and welcome you onto the cliffs of the water's edge, the place where all is well and more and more is becoming available to you (and everyone).

There's something calm about today that we want you to notice and feel today. Once you had a crazy idea that life had to be hard and are now finding out that this doesn't necessarily have to be so.

We're going to take just a moment and float an ancient idea into your beautiful heart and that is that what you want, wants you. You've heard this from us before, but this time we want you to hear this a little differently.

We want you to hear this idea in a fresh, new way, as if you were opening to this idea and this possibility, as if you were hearing it for the first time.

Here's the importance and the truth of this:

You can never have anything you don't already have.

Think about that. You can't have anything you don't already have. What does it mean?

It means, you are everything that matters already. You just forget this and then allow the personality and the ego to gang up on you and try to make you believe otherwise.

What we are trying to say, and we hope you will hear, is you are the chosen one to come forth at this time to live and love as the Christed ones before you.

You are the one who knows no fear as he opens his mind, his heart and his original-ness to the unseen, the unfathomable, and the beautiful that IS in this moment available to you to be seen, felt and experienced.

We want you to know, you can put everything that isn't serving you or coming from you as love into a basket and close the lid where you can let it stew, fester, and never be seen or heard from again.

You are the master who knows what the truth is because you are seeing from the truth mirror where you can indeed see out into the richness of what is, what will be, and what could be, starting right now.

The message to leave you with on this day is this:

One way to live is to survive.

Another way to live is to thrive and to open in each moment as a possibility.

Come quick. You might miss it.

What nonsense?

No reason to stop your spiritual explorations now. Just continue to see and share the truth.

What you want cannot be had without the heart opening required to receive it.

Open now.

Receive as you wish.

The truth has no boundaries.

The truth is something to be welcomed.

The truth is never anything to be feared.

Say your name in a way a disciple who loves you would say your name.

You don't have to run, you don't have to qualify, you don't have to do anything to take on the truth and live from that place.

Truth is your friend.

Always ask for the truth and your growth will be your inevitable companion to your highest version of yourself.

You don't have to do anything to honor the path you are on and the way life embraces you and all your glory.

Believe what you wish for is your natural way of being. Your natural way of opening and your natural way of sightseeing into the clear vision that is being revealed in your favorite moments.

Love yourself. Love the gift of each moment.

Let everything else go that isn't wanted by the truth-seeker inside you.

Blessings to you, oh brilliant one.

You are free of anything that wants to go out and needs to be welcomed in.

Believe it or not, THIS IS a magical day and a magical time. Hold it in the best way possible for what you need is a gift and will always find you.

Much love to you, my friend in the circle.

You are NOT wasting anything. It's all good and it's all on purpose.

Your walk-mate on the path of beautifully delicious love.

Mikela

MESSAGE #34
Living From the "Known"

Dear Love,
What would you have me know today?

Dearest Otto,

We love you and we only want the best for you.

One thing we would have you know today is how lucky you are to be you.

You could have been anyone, but you are you.

Not only are you, you, but you are the one gifted with the insight of clear hearing and clear seeing. You might think those things are traits to be revered or respected or appreciated, but there is one gift you have been gifted with that is even better than those things.

And that is clear knowing.

Clear knowing is being willing to stake your life and stake your future on a feeling that you just "know."

"Knowing" is one of the ultimate gifts.

This gift of "knowing" is so amazing that if you tune into it, pay attention to it, honor it and value it...

This gift will forever change you and honor your path to such a degree that you cannot help but find freedom in the ordinary, love in the complicated and clarity in the foggy and muddy.

What a welcome to the place of truth.

What a remembering of the new way.

What a life made on purpose when you "know" things and you don't question where that insight and knowing came from.

The truth is that it doesn't matter. Life happens and we either fight it or we find the art of flowing with it on the path to honoring the past and cleaning the future.

Our suggestion is this: Don't do anything that would jeopardize that which can never change. It doesn't matter anyway because it's only your thinking about what is real and what is not that can change anything.

Change one thing and everything else changes too.

Now finally, don't be reliant on anything that changes with the wind.

No reason to get excited about anything that doesn't open you, find you in an open space or force you to rethink almost everything, starting right now.

We want you to stay in bliss as you go through life.

Continue to open when you wouldn't want to.

The times are at hand.

The times are at hand.

The times are at hand

Don't waste the times.

Living from your "knowing" is vitally important.

Your knowing is not solid or stagnate. Your "knowing" is a truth that must be honored.

Ask yourself, "What do I know?"

What is the truth?

What way is the way?

Look for what is true. What you know.

Live from the place of what you know, not what you think or what you fear or what your brother or sister says is true.

What do you know?

That is the place to come from.

Live from there.

When you do that, so many unimportant things fall away.

You don't even have to test what you know because it is from a higher place, a deeper place, a place where your wisdom beyond the intellect resides.

The known is what you are present to when the ego loses its grip on you and you go back, go back, go back to who you are, what you are, and how you serve.

The known is a most extraordinary place to live from.

Live from what is known by you.

And it is worth spending some time examining and unveiling what is KNOWN by you.

With love and good feelings for you now and always.

Mikela

MESSAGE #35
A Beautiful Obligation
(Remember to Read This About You)

Dear Love,
What would you have me know about the new job I just applied for?

Dearest Otto,

Why would you ever fear when you know who you are?

On this day you are in for a treat. On this day, you are feeling the after-effects of a high moment, a realization, a walk into a land previously unknown by you in the deepest sense. And this is THE realm of greater possibility.

What you are being faced with in this pursuit is the obligation to claim your highest version of you.

The highest version of you only wants the best for yourself, your brothers and sisters and for the world.

The highest version of you does not react or respond to a possibility with fear, doubt or dread.

The higher version of you ONLY and ALWAYS responds from the deep, abiding miracle of what is and what could be for a soul connected to and opening to the Divine.

When you are focused on the miracle called you living as the Divine, all doubts will wash away like sand being washed off the body by a warm shower as you leave the beach. The focusing on the miracle maintains the miracle of possibility. The washing away of what is not permanent and not wanted for the journey is what is left.

Calm yourself now. Open to the single, solitary thought of who you are.

You are the beloved's son, walking on the earth, living in a body, pretending to not be who he truly is.

To be in the realm of the trusted Divine and in the realm of the sacred is requiring that you shift your personality in ways the personality objects to, and that makes its fears be made more visible to the naked eye like an open wound on an arm or a hand that has been cut.

Now, back to the job in question and the question of your work in this lifetime.

From our perspective, the real question is, what sacred act do you want to do in this life for your financial livelihood at this time?

There is no good or bad or right or wrong.

Your soul's agenda and your soul's purpose will find its own way, no matter what. You do not have to worry if you choose this thing or that thing. You do not have to choose this highway of life or that one.

Your soul, the essence and everlasting aspect of you, will find its own way and will carry your personality with it even if it requires kicking and screaming and pretending to not be who you are.

Revenge of the beggars is the recognition of who you are.

We sense the question of whether you can do this job or not and the answer to this question is of course, YES.

You can.

The only question truly is if you will look to the best parts of this and not the worst parts.

Will you focus on the gift of this or will you focus on your fear?

Will you focus on your patterns or will you focus on the deeper truth of what can be made manifest when you allow the body, mind and the personality to align with your soul?

This whole question that is arising out of fear is only bringing up what is to be healed.

It is only bringing up what has been wanted by you since you were a small body carrying around your infinite, immortal soul.

You entered this incarnation with one thing going for you (as do all beings): You are the son of the Divine and nothing is impossible if you live and love from that place.

Everything is impossible when you don't live from the deeper level, the soul's healthy remembering and sharing of the light and what the light stands for.

The only important thing that must be known about this opportunity, and we do mean opportunity, is what opening to this will really teach you and that teaching is the true power of surrender and the true power of allowing what is wanted to come through.

There is never any such thing as "right timing" or "right answers" to the ego and the personality. They are only about the fear, the negativity and the doubts.

Wake up, brother, to the truth of who you are.

What must be asked at this time is do you want to keep going down the path you are on or do you want to surrender to the Divine track that is being prepared.

You very often fight this idea but we keep bringing you back again and again to the essence of the moment and the question at hand.

Will you choose to grow or will you choose to step out of someone else's drama and let someone else step in?

You can either get the lesson now or you can take the train to another station where the ticket for the lesson will be handed out on another stop.

The lesson is about loving yourself, challenging yourself and loving life.

Make no mistake, this will bring up many aspects of self-healing that must be undertaken and forgiven but you are up for it, my wise and intuitive friend.

You can make the claim now and step into your divinity now and leave all aspects of the fearful follower behind if you like. We will beckon you into the highest aspects of yourself if you choose.

Will you choose the path you've been on (even after you've gotten the lesson) or will you release the resistance to your best, highest self in this the morning of the sacred life of the one known as Otto?

You can learn this or anything as long as you know, remember and live from the truth of who you are and the aspects of you and your being that never ever changes.

Believe, dear brother. Believe in the miracle known as you.

Own your divinity. Own your right to your place in the sun.

The real problem is you are having a spiritual temper tantrum and you don't want to get up off the floor and be the adult aspect of you instead of the child that got left behind (in its way of seeing the world).

Again, we say, wake up. Wake up. Wake up.

You can do this. The only question is, do you want to.

Do you want to grow in this way or do you want to choose to stay frozen in your previous path to healing?

We will help you come to this with a fresh way of seeing and being.

Clear out the fear, clear out the judgments of yourself and what used to be, and what you used to be like, and say YES to a new feeling within.

We said it before:

The time and the healing is quickening.

The fear doesn't have to report for duty in a life where it's no longer needed.

Walk in the light where the pathway is being lit before you.

Accept the easy path rather than the hard path and this counsel applies to all matters where the fears have raised their ugly heads again wanting to be heard.

Do not give unhealthy fears a voice.

Give them a back seat and tape their mouths shut.

Blessing be to you, our famous Butterfly.

We love you and hope this has served you today.

May you open as love in this and all moments especially with yourself.

Your friend in the Spirit,

Mikela

MESSAGE #36

The Demands of Your Essence

Dear Love,
What would you have me know today?

Dearest Otto,

You are a seeker, aren't you? You love and you bring your love with you wherever you go in this world. It's a blessing to the ones who enter your path in life.

What we would have you know today is how truly loved you are at each step along the way in your life journey.

You pretend that you don't know this but it's time you recognize the truth of who you are.

You are the one sent here at this time to be a way-shower and a disciple of the Christ to stand firm in your conviction that love is what truly matters and a life isn't really well lived if you haven't seen how much love matters and how there is nothing to fear and nothing to consider when you come to the choice of opening or closing your heart in the here and now.

What is so strange within you and in your life is how attached you are to making yourself small and making yourself out to be a victim of some kind when the manifestation you seek is but a heartbeat away when you see, know and own the truth of who you are.

Wait for it...

The messages are coming in clear. You cannot waste a life when you see what the truth is. So, you must not see the truth yet. Or, you must at least be unwilling to see the truth in a way that opens you deeper and deeper into the space of love and a legendary commitment to living as a Divine instrument, living and breathing as love in all your moments.

The reason we're bringing this to the surface is that you are not owning your true essence and your true beingness as it relates to your life that appears to be less than its capabilities and less than is possible at this time.

What if the only thing you needed to do to have more of the life you want is to own the life you've got fully and completely and agree to have the rhythm of life turn more in your favor than let you believe you are less than well, anything.

One thing matters here...

Will you claim your Divine essence or will you continue down the road of being less than who you truly are?

Just place a little diagram in your shoe if you forget the truth of who you are and look at it if you have too. But you don't have to hide from anyone or anything. The essence of who you are demands you love yourself and love your life in these turbulent times we live in.

We urge you to find the claim form and sign your name to it as an acknowledgment of acceptance of the truth of who you are.

The fathers and mothers that visit on occasion are very proud of you but you're going to want and need to step up, step up, step up.

Fill your energy field and your aura with the essence of who you are and you'll never worry for anything ever again.

Claim your heart, claim your goodness and most importantly... claim your reason for coming here—which is to love yourself even when others don't. It's to love yourself when you can't see the way forward too.

All it takes is being willing to claim your ownership of the truth of who you are—and the rest is history.

You then, are the witness to the last frontier being claimed and that is the last frontier of willingness to own who you are.

Claim who you are right now. Claim what is rightfully yours. Claim the truth and never forget how you got here.

And that claim is the essence that is named ALL ONE will be the switchover from not knowing one moment and fully knowing the next.

Take a good look. The mountains are waiting for you to arrive and there is calm in the air.

You won't need a jacket because you know what your limits truly are and how they serve you.

But limits aren't the problem anymore.

It's being willing to be the one who stands in his center and roars like the head of the lion to make his point.

But you don't want to be located within the mansion because of how you perceive how you can come home to the truth of who you are...right here and right now.

Welcome the true essence of who you are and let it out into the world with the same subtlety of a herd of buffalo running in step with the big, giant herd.

It's as easy as it will be. And that is fulfillment of the wishes and desires of the one named Otto in human form.

Don't run from the path you are on. Embrace it fully and completely.

Own your essence. Live your life. Love everyone who enters your path.

Especially do whatever it takes to love yourself and then spread that love in the world.

Many blessings to you.

Your spokesperson for the Divine love in all things.

Mikela

MESSAGE #37
Mikela on Forgiveness

Dear Love,
What would you have me know about forgiveness?

Dearest Otto,

Wait for it and it will be gone. Rush to it and it will not come closer. Invite it on the other hand, and it will flow to you effortlessly.

What an interesting topic you have selected for us today.

And while we are grateful you are here, we must ask, "Where have you been?" We have been wondering where you have eloped to. Where have you sheltered yourself? What has kept you from the learning that is yours to do?

We see you in all your glory and kindly offer a new possibility that is not available from the mindless drivel on the so-called world wide web. Take advantage of the lessons and possibilities being given so freely. We promise it is (and will be) time well spent.

As for your asking about forgiveness and what we would have you know about this lost art and its role in not only your life but the lives of most of God's creations in the human realm...

It will be a brief but very important distinction.

Forgiveness is not a tool. It is an act of love for yourself and an act of love for not only your brothers and sisters but all beings who stand in their innocence and wish things were different and they are not. Forgiveness is the freedom filter to the fresh new dawn that can only be seen with fresh new eyes that appear once the murkiness has been lifted from the main thread that is connected to your fear and your doubts and your struggle that MUST be released once and for all if you are to enter the new world within.

What can frustrate you and tie your energy up like a braided under-the-ocean cable is not the thing that has you tied up in a ball but your reaction to it and your fear of it.

We're not talking about the fear of the thing, the event or the situation. We're talking about the fear that arises when there is a thought (a very innocent thought) that you have focused on that brings you from the edge of darkness to the lip of the portal that ushers in the light that you refuse and send back to the hole in your heart and the portal of fear in your heart that gets closed and unable to let in the extreme beauty that is waiting to be offered and presented to the world.

Shake the tree, dear brother, and watch the fruit fall into your largest bucket that you will carry with you to the gathering place where the true essence breaks free and breaks apart from the wisdom that gets it to THIS place where we now sit.

There is nothing to fear here but you make up the stories that there is and we remind you that anything (as your friend Peter suggests) is "just an idea" and those ideas are no better than the ones that come to you in the middle of the night when all good servants are in their sleep and slumber time.

What if there was never a need for forgiveness in the early part of the day that is full of promise. And surely you can see that there is never a need for forgiveness in the outer realm as well. Stay right here and welcome the truth in all matters for the truth is a tiny error that was believed and made real for a moment, for an hour or a life time and it is truly not necessary unless you are committed to holding on to that which does NOT serve you in the highest way possible.

What good is believing a false truth that will one day be found out—the truth that you are the Christ, you are the innocent one, you are made of that which can never be broken.

Brother, Sister, begin with a new intention to rest in the day's work that has yet to be finished. It has yet to be finished because no one wants a crying baby at the fishbowl tournament routinely measured in the light being allowed in.

We're going to make an offer to you right now that (if you accept) could come in the form of an energetic awakening. But it will be like opening the fire door and pulling out the ashes from the old, the dying, the complex and the witness that wishes to be offered the plan to being reborn in an instant without fear, without anything that is being picked up for future use in the social store.

Forgiveness is the one rotten piece of bread that's left over that no one wants to eat. It's not something that is fresh. It's not a prize to be auctioned off that was left over after all was being forgotten and forgiven.

Forgiveness is a beautiful tool that breaks up the hardened energy that's left over from a fall energetically from the mountain where the truth of what is is written down.

Forgiveness is always done for you and not for another. Forgiveness is not done to hedge your bets in the life of a free one with cloudy thinking and a painful residue left as a reminder of who we are not as the world rotates in its perfect orbit and perfect harmony.

Do not be afraid to capture the moment forgiveness is trying to block us from having.

Forgiveness is always to be released in accordance with what is not wanted. What is not poised for the new dawning of peace in the mind's eye.

Leadership is impossible without forgiveness. Love, true love, is not possible while waiting for the dew to fall from the leaves and the trees. Love, like forgiveness, must be active and without hesitation. For what is being honored, blessed and relived over and over must be cleared for the best, freest life possible.

Forgiveness is NOT one and done.

Forgiveness is a practice that must start with the intention to never stop, O' innocent one.

Find the power inside for the one moment when the art of forgiveness rains down on you and sets you free (literally) to have, be or do anything in the energy and Divine spark of this one creation that you sometimes have trouble claiming the beauty of.

Walk with me to the other side where all the forgiveness blows you away at the frequency that is the forgiveness frequency. Wake up to the freedom, the wealth and the life that only wants the best version of you to show up. It cannot do so if there is so much still remaining to be forgiven.

Make forgiveness first and all other things second because forgiveness is the roadblock to freedom, power and abundance (in all ways.)

It's hard to see at first, but the role of forgiveness is the releasing of the brakes that hold you in place and keep you stuck when you need not be.

Forgive yourself for everything right here, right now. There's no shortcut to the freedom you seek. Forgiveness is one of the doorways to the Divine in you, in me and in everyone.

You just choose to make forgiveness more of a boulder than you can carry by yourself because you try to pick it up in one fell swoop and all by yourself.

Raise your hands to the heavens and breathe into the majesty of a life without pain, stuckness and suffering.

Forgiveness is one of these ways.

But for heaven's sake, take the best from others but make your forgiveness practice your own and use whatever form rings as truth for YOU.

Not anyone else. Just YOU.

A future without forgiveness is a future stuck in the past and that is NOT a fancy place to create from at all.

Blessings to you, my famous butterfly.

We're glad you're back for the lessons.

You are innocent. You are whole. You are forgiven. You are loved.

Freedom to live and freedom to create waits for you on the other side of the gift of forgiveness.

Forgive yourself for everything.

Start now in this very moment by saying...

"I forgive myself for judging myself as anything less than whole, complete and perfect."

I am the Word.

And so are you, my brother.

Don't ever think you are not.

Blessings to you.

Mikela.

MESSAGE #38
Integrity and the Truth of What Is
(Remember to Read This About You)

Dear Love,
What would you have me know about my current job?

Dearest Otto --

We love you and we honor you in this moment and in all moments.

What we would have you know about your current job is it's toxic.

It's toxic because it is out of integrity with who you are and who you are moving toward.

This job has served you well. It has gotten you out of debt completely once. It's taught you about money (that was the goal wasn't it?) and it has shown you about abundance and wealth. At the same time, it has shown you about wealthy people (in financial terms) and not-so-wealthy people and how the amount of money you have in the bank or in investments has NOTHING to do with your personal happiness and everything to do with being clear about how you see yourself, how you see other people and how you see life's many possibilities.

Take heed, my brother, and notice how you are now...only there out of obligation and commitment to not a job really but an idea about what this job gives you which is safety and prison. It's safe because you are assured to get that pay every two weeks and it's a prison because you are trapped in an idea that you can't do anything else and you can't win at anything else at this "late stage of life."

How ridiculous!

There's no such thing as a job giving you safety and protection. Safety and protection are only concepts and ideas that someone made up to stoke the fires of fear and have you give in to a mentality of quitting and giving in.

It's time to stop all this nonsense.

This job is no longer serving you. It is no longer stretching you and is no longer demanding you bring out your best.

But this lack of bringing out your best is NOT happening by accident. It is happening because of an integrity breach about debt, what's right and what you believe is good, healthy and right for another brother or sister who wishes to sit in the sun and open to the best life possible for them.

It's about wanting to see, truly see, the best for everyone and the belief you hold that debt really does force you to spend more than you would otherwise. It's also about reconciling your belief that debt really does make you lose sight of all consciousness about spending, saving and what these things can undo in a life that longs for more and is still struggling to raise his income to into a higher level of abundance.

So...

There are two factors at play here.

There is the toxic work environment and there is the integrity piece.

So, let's do you a favor and shortcut this "who" thing...

You can't be in integrity with yourself and what is true for most people if you are living a workplace lie that isn't about love. isn't about integrity and isn't about truly being agenda-less. Can you?

We stand here claiming the light that you need to be illumined in and bathed in. You can and should find the overlap between integrity and being in a job and a career that best serves without fear and without bias for good.

Don't let anything get in the way of your living in your integrity.

Everything else depends on it.

Your love, your leadership and most of all, your health depends on BEING in integrity with the truth of what is.

Create a life in integrity with the truth of who you are and the rest is easy.

This place is NOT that.

It is a negative 25 on the understanding scale that waits for the truth to be revealed and the truth to be understood and the truth to be lived.

Let's go.

Demand more from yourself than you are currently demanding and the truth of who you are will naturally shine more and more of the time.

And this, my friend, is a good thing.

You gotta get out while you're young.

The rest of your life (in beautiful harmony) is waiting on your welcome.

Integrity is your friend and your growth partner.

Be well and be blessed.

Your friend,

Mikela

MESSAGE #39

That's All It Takes

Dear Love,
What would you have me know today?

Dearest Otto,

We greet you on the first day of the rest of your life in wholeness and gratitude. You are the gift you seek outside of yourself already in manifested form.

Many see this and in time...perhaps today...in 5 minutes, 5 days or 5 years, you will make the most loving and profound choice. And that choice is to love yourself fully and completely with no regrets for your sins of the past and no fears of the future you wish to create.

The only thing we would have you know today is how much you have available to you as you stand in your center and see your choices fully and say YES to those choices that serve you and your fellow man in beautiful ways.

The key is choice.

Choice in how you create yourself.

Choice in how you love yourself.

Choice in how you see the world and how you see the other players that show up in your little life drama called earth school.

You are rich beyond measure and gifted beyond measure in these troubling times and we trust that you are beginning to see the truth of this more and more in each passing moment and with each passing thought.

Nowhere does it say that you can't heal, learn and grow in this lifetime AND manifest in ways that are of your liking and of your wanting too.

See into the mirror the reflection of the one before you known as you--the one baffled by the truth and believer of his fears (at least up until now) and love the one reflected back to you no matter what judgements have been made by you and others about the one before you in the mirror.

All we would have you know in this moment is:

You have everything you need now and always to move mountains and stop the voice that doesn't serve your highest good and fall into the healing waters laid out for you as your gift from the eternal one known by some as the Creator, by others as the Beloved and by others as the one true timeless Spirit.

The juxtaposition of your focus and what is wanted, along with the understanding, the commitment and welcoming of the truth of who you are in this time of wrestling with your judgements of old and new—

Are causing you to feel stuck and feel like you're not getting any traction toward the goals you've set for yourself.

Stop it. Stop it. Stop it.

Open your possibility journal to the first page and write a possibility down for you that would be awesome and then...

Love yourself enough to create that in this moment...first in your belief zone in your mind and then in your reality as your belief takes hold enough.

That's all it takes...to love yourself enough that you stop believing anything that doesn't reinforce and recreate the master you are in human form and then...you create your masterpiece of a life from that place.

It's healthy to love yourself and it's a companion to the beliefs that reward you in this lifetime—not in the future but now for deciding to say a full-bodied YES to the teachings you have drifted away from as you struggled to live from your own lies and independent state.

Match the frequency of the Beloved and LOVE yourself without ceasing. Love yourself enough that it shines through to all your decisions and all your interactions in this world.

It's time for you to stand in your full glory and walk tall and full of the spirit that sent you here, starting now. And now. And now.

Much love to you always, junior.

Mikela

MESSAGE #40
Shine

Dear Love,
What would you have me know today?

Dear Otto--

We feel your welcome this day and are so appreciative of who you are and your openness and your willingness to explore deeply with us.

It is a grand day. So grand in fact, that you can see the Sun shining through the clouds, through the disarray, through the disharmony within and without.

What we would have you know today is...

Everything is Perfect.

How could it not be?

Once upon a time, there were transmitters of energy in your midst and they had only one job—to transmit energy and light and open the hearts of others. You are one of those beings. You just haven't accepted this fact.

You move around the earth plane without vision and without commitment to the healing needed within you and in your requirement to transmit healing to others through only the nature of your being.

With only a tool such as your voice—the greatest of all your gifts, you could open the hearts of thousands (or millions) if you so choose.

BUT, the doubts and the unclaimed victory has kept you from the palace and kept you from the kingdom that you have initiated from. Now you get to see, through the ones sent to you, how much pain we can all create when we don't see our own Divinity and live from the truth of that.

The moment at hand is painful because you are in transition. You are in transition from thinker to believer to knower. The transition is happening quickly and the power of this cannot be understated.

You, of all people, should see through the glass and out the other end about the strands of energy that permeate all beings and how this is a time of great transition for not only you, but all beings at this time.

The prerequisite for the healing that MUST take place is the settling in, the softening and some might say—the loving toward yourself and toward others—as the beams of light begin to be unsheathed and taken out from under their coverings and begin to be not only shown, but known in the world in ways unseen before now.

A little freedom can go a long way and the gift of freedom is where the openings are to the doorway known as "the beautiful flow."

The "beautiful flow" is almost as clear as the energy that melts on contact but it is designed to flow through and around those installed with the light and the willingness to put down their shields and herald the shift for others that need a fresh, new beginning in the here and now (sometimes known as the present moment).

What good can come of waiting until the last moment to make a decision that can change a life?

What good can come from "testing" the frequency of fear VS trust...heartache VS an open willingness to see situations as gifts and teachers instead of misery collectors?

We want you to forget everything you have ever known that was not a direct line to the truth and a direct line to energy fortification within you and the others you teach and will be teaching.

Trust ONLY in the truth and you can only find the truth in the well of unwavering bliss, the well of unwavering beauty and the well of unwavering freedom.

You have to trust what is being offered. You have to trust where you are. The way is being paved.

Settle in to IT.

The way is being offered not because you are anything unique or special any more than anyone else is unique or special. The way being offered is a gift that must be brought at this time and you are the one to bring it.

We want you to own the truth from this moment on and be a willing sharer of this that you will be given.

If you stay only in truth, stay only in the power of love and in the power issued by the one known by many as the creator of all things, you will allow the fear that comes up to be seen always and immediately for what it is and shake it off and move forward in certainty of the task you are being given.

The task is as follows:

Use the last quarter of your life for your own healing and the healing of others.

Remember the directive we have proclaimed to you many times. There is never a reason to fear. Ever.

That is your work to see beginning right now.

There is never a reason to fear. Ever.

Take that and have it be your guide. For a single breath is all that may be needed to free yourself and others from any untruth that darkens the way or casts a shadow over their light that so desperately wants to shine.

Wherever you go, come only in love and bring your most powerful flashlight.

Shine, Dear Brother.

Shine.

Show others how to shine as well.

Love is the greatest force in the universe.

Come only as love.

Love, first for yourself and love for others.

That is all.

Show up and shine.

Show up and open your heart.

Show up and revisit the truth often for others are depending on the light that is needed to show them the way forward.

Love without fear.

Love without ceasing.

Say hello to beauty as this is your new focus, the focus of love and beauty recognition.

Bring any believer along with you as a teacher and a way shower as the needs are plenty in this time of great confusion of purpose and desires.

Holy instants are to be recognized by you more quickly and the way to do that is to be on constant lookout over the horizon and spot the teachings and the gifts that are to be shared.

Will has nothing to do with this.

This is an assignment—to cast only love and show up only as love.

It starts with you and your willingness to offer up what will be sent to you.

No bravery needed. No sacrifice needed.

Only surrender.

And love.

Be well, my beautiful friend.

Until next time.

Much love to you,

Mikela

MESSAGE #41

Would You?

Dear Love,
What would you have me know today?

Dearest Otto --

We greet you with love and an open heart for good things are happening. We love that you are seeing life in new ways even in the midst of great change and turmoil in yourself and the world.

Would you help a brother or a sister?

Would you?

The answer to this question is all you need to know about your place and your value in the world.

This question of whether you would help a brother or a sister is both a very simple one and a very complex one at the same time. It's simple because it is fairly straightforward and it's complex because you, like most people, put so many "buts" and "what ifs" in front of this question that it's hard to know what your real answer to this question would truly be.

Would you help a brother or a sister? Is the only requirement for choosing a life of service.

But that's not quite strong enough. An even better question would be, "Will you help a brother or a sister?"

This is the prerequisite for knowing whether your belt needs to be tightened and your arms unfolded as you wait at the doorstop for the next assignment to love a brother or a sister in your own unique way that only you can.

Will you take responsibility for making sure the door to your heart stays open and the great news is shared with not only those wanting the first crack at the certainty of life but those who are not casual about life, love, and the freedom waiting on the other side of being true to you?

We want you to spend just a few moments breathing in and breathing out the perfect unfolding of your favorite life and find that image that means so much to you and clutch it to your breast and repeat after me...

"I am a soul companion for those who enter my path seeking new ways to live life and hoping to find the certainty of slowing down in their normal days, weeks and years. I am the window of freedom so many desire. I am the one designed to shower others with kindness, love and a healthy dose of the truth and possibilities that opens them to the right moment to share their destiny with ease, grace and flow."

We know you are wanting some special insights into how you and your mate are to conduct yourselves so you can maximize the impact you create in your upcoming trip to your conference.

And to that we would simply say...

Just go be in truth and just go be light.

Share these two things until you can't share anymore.

Honor yourselves and honor your most beloved on high with the news you've been waiting for which is on full display in the heart of roses—the place where love dwells within you that cannot be mistaken for something else that comes out of the mouth of the false prophets and teachers that would take you sideways instead of forward.

Listen in the silence while the morning light is being ushered in.

Listen in the wind for the next set of instructions that should be coming your way soon.

Don't hesitate to play matchmaker with what you bring to a party, which is the gift of insight, the gift of love, and the gift of seeing what is needed.

Don't look for the damaged goods. Look only for the train in motion and going forward toward the beautiful vista you see outward as your full manifestation comes into view.

Look for the pure, the innocent and the wanting that enters your life in normal and strange ways to see in them and to share with them the possibilities that are on offer.

No reason to come here with treats no one can eat.

Come here standing in your faith and in your love and watch these beautiful beings that cross your path and notice when it's in a space where they're really ready, and then offer them what they want...

A soft, peaceful feeling that never changes and never gets old.

In closing, one last thing we want to say is this:

Never focus on what's wrong when you could focus on their perfection being manifested in human form right in front of you.

This is true for every human you'll ever come in contact with.

They want something that's already inside them that they can't see.

Your job is to help them see the truth of who and what they are in the most direct, simple, and loving way possible.

We wish you the sun, the moon, and the stars as you embark on your path laid out for you in the most perfect of ways.

Travel safe distances with the grace freely given to you as you settle in to a path like no other and a path of pure love.

Until next time.

And whatever you do, hold yourself and your ideals lightly.

You'll be better served to create your life from that place than its opposite.

Your friend in the spirit world.

Mikela

MESSAGE #42
Required: A White-Hot Desire

Dear Love,
What would you have me know about creating a highly
profitable and financially sustainable business teaching people
how to create the love they really want and helping people
see and live from the truth of who they really are, not at a
personality level, but a soul level?

Dearest Otto,

We have missed you and our connection in the late hour of the evening and wish nothing but the best for you and know that the best for you will be helped by our connection and the bridge we form to connecting deeper to the Divine.

There is only one thing standing in the way of your full embodiment of this desire of yours and that is a white-hot desire that usurps all other petty desires not in alignment with the truth of who you are and what you are capable of, creating in the lover's portal and the soul's connection with the Divine.

Nothing can keep you from having what you want except for the fear of what will happen if you go for this great desire of yours and your fear of what it will take to manifest this in broad daylight, with everyone watching in full view of the show taking place that only creates love and a soul's growth to the end of the earth and back without wanting anything in return except for the knowing of a job well done and you becoming who you would have to BE to accomplish all that would be required to manifest this in your full glory.

Let us repeat that, a white-hot desire, so full of the passion and so full of the level of BEING and the level of service required that would literally force, in a loving way, the creation of the lover's march to glory in the remainder of this one lifetime.

One day and one moment is all it takes to give up the fear, the doubt, and the waiting and the unfolding of the arms and the opening of the heart. It's the one thing that will override all other opportunities for running in place, staying stuck and allowing your fears to sideline you from playing the game of your life. AND that game is the game of life and love creation from a place of witnessing the miracle of truth and love in action.

Why wait for any type of permission?

You get to decide how you will live.

You get to decide how you will move forward.

You get one crack at the manifestation of the lovers in full view of all who enter the doorway to love, and then it's much harder to keep everything still enough to operate without fear leading the way.

Ice is one way to create fresh and new, and another way is to show how simple it really is to be born again in the spiritual realm where the #1 thing you could ever know is how there is nothing to fear. Ever.

Take your time and wish upon your nearest star your greatest desire, and the one after that and the one after that, and you will be surprised at how simple it is to shift who you are being when you are committed to who you are being.

Never is it a good idea to take one doorway and put the lock on it so not only could the good stuff not get out, but the good stuff couldn't get in either.

Push beyond what you think is possible and the results will start to show in short order.

We say pushing as a metaphor due to the fact that there's no pushing needed when you invite men and women to the bounty known as their life when they create from a safe, warm, and dry place away from the painful stories they have believed up until now.

There will be the type of images normally reserved for the wise ones, but now you are waking up to the fact that you are one of the wise ones, and you are the one that carries the special offer in his wallet that can be redeemed at full value at any time.

"Act as if" is not just a pretty little saying. It is the backbone of desiring that which you desire, that which is only being offered to you.

It's time to witness a sea-turtle's nest full of want-to and the will to go even slower in your quest for freedom, love and truth.

It's time to put some more meat in the pot and stir it around to avoid it getting too hot. It's time for you to understand that life can become messy and it's OK to get in on the fun while the sun is shining.

Tend to your physical body in tandem with your spiritual body and what they both need, and your results will be remarkable.

Your soul will be campaigning for the right to shift in any way it chooses that would be for its highest good.

There is NO WEAKNESS and no perception needed as you enter the different landscape you have called to you.

There is only what you have called to you in the imprint of the soul's castle and the soul's journey that really matters.

There's no reason to fake left and fake right in your quest to go all the way when the window of time needed is seconds on the dinner line and playfulness in the humor line.

The quest can be over as soon as the fear drops away. There is no reason to wager from the workplace when there are so many other options to choose from.

Just drop the fear and open your heart to the space where certainty dwells in every moment and you can create anything from that place.

Just place a loving command in your heart and set anything else free that gets in the way of the thing you want that wants you.

Blessings be now through reunion day.

You are resilient, you are loved, and you are unstoppable.

It's time to act like it.

Your friend in the spirit world.

Mikela

MESSAGE #43

The Most Important Being That Ever Existed

Dear Love,
What would you have me know today?

Dearest Otto,

We want you to know that you are doing excellent work right now. We want you to know you are clearing five thousand years of fear and lostness in this time and space and throughout the remainder of this year. We also want you to know that more important than anything we could ever tell you, we want to share with you once again how deeply loved and how deeply connected you are to the Divine, and how deeply you are connected to the Divine spark in everyone you meet.

Here's something you may not know...

There is a match going on right now where you are being matched up with another being who will guide you to the next phase of your life. This match isn't like a match on a dating app or anything like that. This "match" was predestined from the time before you were born to carry you into the next phase of your life and into the light where you will recognize ALL things you see but don't notice, you hear but don't recall and you think about but don't know yet.

This, my friend, is the right path in the right way that is being blended especially for you in the heart space you remember and cherish. This is the heart space of total and unconditional love.

This is waiting for you now.

All you have to do is be willing to receive and be willing to open your heart to the new ways of living and serving. These new ways of living and serving are not anything to be fearful of. Quite the opposite. This new guide and these new teachings will be sharing the new truth and working with you on nothing more than the necessary releasing of the addictive ways of thinking, seeing and being that is NOT in accord with the higher laws and your highest level of consciousness available to you now.

One day there will be no complaints. One day there will be no chance for what you might call "failure" because from here on out, there is no such thing as "failure."

You will begin to see this as you continue working on your list of judgments you are working so hard to release and let go of. THIS is the place where nothing in the world can save you because there is nothing to be saved from. There is only the mystery that wakes you up at night and the mystery that guides your every move.

One day, there will be no more talk of fear, doubt and insecurity as we know in our heart of hearts that there is no mystery in what is wanted and what is needed for the journey home.

You are not ready for the journey yet. There is much to be done by you and the ones who will enter your path in the doorway to the Divine, also known as the trusting and loving way.

Whatever is going through your mind, just know that the journey isn't complete yet. We implore you to trust in the Divine and look through the Divine doorway.

Balk at anything not necessary for the journey ahead. Tune into what is wanted, what is needed, and what has been asked for.

Please know that whatever you want or need will always be supplied. Whatever you require is on the frame below the wishing well.

Now, you are ready to begin ushering in the new dawn that we have been teasing you with for the past several months.

You are stepping up to the infinite and you are one of a kind.

You are about to re-member the truth of who you are. And this is the most important awakening of your journey right now, the remembering of the TRUTH of who you are.

This is the wisdom required in the morning and the truth required in the evening to work in the present moment on this most important thing, YOU.

You are the most important BEING that has ever existed. You need to find the places where that is true and live from those places.

We are filled with so much gratitude and love for you.

We love you and we look forward to the next interaction in this current form.

You're doing great. Do NOT allow even one thought that reinforces any negative aspect of you.

You are a light being, a bringer of the dawn, and a wonderful soul with a Divine purpose.

Share this only if you make the decision to carry your beautiful message forward.

Much love to you, my friend.

Mikela

MESSAGE #44
No Time for Playing Small

Dear Love,
What would you have me know today?

Dearest Otto,

You are a peach of a guy. Bet you haven't heard anyone say that to you in a while, have you? A peach of a guy you are indeed. But, let's not forget how splendid you are, how wonderful it is to have you here, and how utterly poignant this moment is in your life. We love you and respect and appreciate what you bring to the world.

What we would have you know today is a bounce back from the past of sorts. We're calling it a "bounce-back" because there have been times in your life when you have felt like an unstoppable king, a confident master, or a cocky visitor in your life and the lives of the ones before you.

This is so important to remember, even if it is only for a split second. It's important to allow yourself to go back in time and find one place, two places, or a hundred thousand places where you felt like you "belonged," you were confident, and you deserved to be in the conversation of living and creating from a place of being "fully alive" and fully certain that you were deserving of whatever the moment was going to bring you, and you knew that would be good.

What if you would take a stand for you, your confidence, and your gifts, and really saw them as right, real, and vital to the one before you?

What if you could eliminate any and all negative judgment about your worth as a soul, as a human being, or as one devoted to being in his amazingness? What if you could just spring forth from complete aliveness and sprout the energy from deep inside that is always there and always waiting to be released but your fears, doubts, and old ways of thinking and believing throw the bricks in front of the tires of the car? What if you have chosen to let a few blocks or barriers keep you from the manifestation of the Divine kingdom that is rightfully yours to live out for the rest of your days?

Let's take a quick moment and sprinkle gratitude dust on the heart area of your inner being, and then, let's take a moment and spring forth into action and guide yourself to one particular place within, the place where the candle cannot be blown out and the place inside where the light can never go dim and the wisdom and soul connection starts to rise up from within and inform you of your next right action. And that next right action is nothing more and nothing less than to claim the truth of who you are, to claim all the goodness from within and all the magic destined to come from the most important place of all, your inner being that is connected to the ALL that is.

Imagine there was a vehicle that was yours to cart you around in but it was made of pure gold and you choose most of the time to take the rickshaw instead of the gold-lined and gold-plated vehicle that is designed to honor and bestow the gifts of forever in the moment of now. You see in a flash that you've come to NOT accept the truth of who you are but you are told to wait. Wait, wait for the mirror of truth that is nothing more than that and it inflicts a brown mist into the area of stars near and around you and you get a glimpse of the truth of who you are so deeply, so profoundly, and from such a place of an invitation that you finally do get a real, true glimpse of radical perfection in human form, destined to come forth and produce more fruit that he could ever have imagined.

But the producing of fruit is a small, yet simple, metaphor for life.

You are gifted with a Divine energy and a Divine consciousness that anyone can notice from a hundred miles away that must be heard, felt, seen, and experienced by others.

All we wish to say to you is this:

Do not hide any more.

There is no time for hiding from this point on. There is no place for doubt from here on out, and there is certainly no room for fear of anyone or anything, beginning now and for the rest of your days.

Climb to the top of the wagon and look out at the fresh, new world that is yet undiscovered by you or anyone and invite yourself and invite your brothers and sisters to claim their best, highest selves and never again take a stand for anything NOT in alignment with the truth of who you are.

A true miracle is waiting to be expressed in full bloom and full capacity of showing up with your brightest flashlight, and shining the way on the path for others to see and to walk on.

Just one inkling, just one thought of the truth, just one powerful moment of recognizing the 28 ways of wisdom that can come to visit when there's nothing in the way or nothing to block the flow of life force that's dying to come out and live fully and completely.

Dear Otto, come with us to the garden and sprinkle some seeds of greatness and some seeds of truth over the grave of the man still alive and beckon him to spring to life.

Nothing is too tough, too big of a task and nothing to be afraid of as you are offered up the golden robe to wear as you enter the land of possibility known as your life. When you take the brakes off and grab onto the reins of strength, wisdom, and purpose and allow yourself to open for the broadcast straight from the Source and the higher self, you are set free to do not just the work that is to be done, but to open to the fun that could be had when you lay ALL your burdens down and only speak truth.

This is the moment when the miracles in your life are truly set free and are then allowed to roam about in the wilderness of the "I am worthy of the love I desire and the manifestations not yet realized" playground and say a full-bodied YES to the life on offer for you.

It's not time to play small. It's time to act like you are the son (or daughter) of the One and fear not anything that is subject to the comings and goings of life and to say YES to the gift that you are.

Why not say YES to it all?

Your life awaits.

Blessings to you, my friend. We welcome you to the life of pleasure and deservedness.

Happy birthday early.

You are wonderful.

Love is the answer always and in ALL WAYS.

Talk to you soon.

Your friend from the spirit world.

Mikela

MESSAGE #45

One Thing You Should Never Deny

Dear Love,
What would you have me know today?

Dearest Otto,

You have come such a long way in just a short time and we are so proud and excited to witness who you are and who you are becoming.

Who you are is a simple man in a simple dream wanting things that don't belong to him, and he can't see this clearly yet.

What are we trying to say here?

In every man's life, there are things that belong to him, things that are for him, things that are so much a part of his being that he is so naturally drawn to them that he can't resist them, he can't hide from them, and he surely can't forget them.

These are the things that show up in his life that are "must lessons." And by this we mean things you MUST have as a part of your life that you must encounter, must dance with, which could also be called situations or people, that guarantee that he "get" the lesson he was meant to get in this lifetime.

You have been going through some of these things in full beauty lately and at a certain level, it has not been fun or enjoyable at all. And on the other hand, these life situations and people are mandates for "getting" a certain life lesson, "getting" certain ways of being, and "getting" certain life answers that you wouldn't have been able to "get" otherwise.

Would you have liked for these so-called lessons to have come in easier, more enjoyable, or more pleasing ways?

Of course, you would have.

But that way of "getting" certain lessons is for another time and a different set of lessons in different circumstances.

In this space and time, the perfect life and the perfect way to "get" the lesson, and the perfect way to grow, to change, and to evolve into the highest version of yourself is right here, in this moment, right where it has always been.

By the time you are done with this current set of life lessons, you will have gained so much and who could blame you if you felt a little, or maybe a lot, tired and weary and crave to just go somewhere and put your feet up and look out at the hot sun and feel the warm breeze on your face for a good while.

But that will come soon.

But first, a decision.

We see that you are faced with a decision about whether to stand up and be counted, or whether you are going to step into a small room, shut the door behind you, and metaphorically pull down the blinds and not step out of the room and into your greatness.

Will you do us this one favor?

Drill a large hole through the main door that faces the path that calls to you in the daylight and in your dreamtime and all the hours in-between. For what you will see when you look through that hole in the main door is the view of the vista that is possible for you in your now and in your future.

Now, in this moment, find the good places within you that you totally and completely approve of and live and love into those places like there is no tomorrow. And this is because there is no tomorrow and there is no future, and there is no place out there that is better, more powerful or more alive than THIS moment and THIS time right here.

Let's tap into the best you have to offer and say goodbye to any speck of doubt, inferiority, hurt, or disappointment that remains inside you from anywhere and anytime and lay it all down like you would lay down burning hot coals that just came from the past and came from anywhere that no longer means anything to you.

Love is the place to come from in all circumstances and in all ways.

Do NOT let the memories of the painful past cloud your vision of what is possible when you live and love from the true place of who you are.

Once there was a time you believed you could do anything. It's time to bring that feeling back. It's time to see a new way. And it's time to see a new star arising in you.

None of this is intended to shift you in unhealthy or ego-filled ways. It is all designed to lift you into the highest, most loving, and most complete version of yourself.

Once was enough pain to experience in a single lifetime and now you can play with the delights of a drama-free life and a whole lotta giving and receiving as we head into the final round up that must be seen and experienced. "Giving and receiving" is the way it should be and the twin sides of the same coin that abides in perfect harmony with the stone that never gets thrown, the blame that never gets assigned, or the missing friend that you wish you still had.

One more time and one more moment is all you ever need to make THIS moment stand out and BE the best moment of all time.

In time, everything you need to feel to open the doorway you most need is available to you without the need to even ask for it.

The thing you most need always comes and it always comes in perfect timing and perfect harmony with what is needed in the moment.

Share with someone you love today what it means to you to have them in your life, and share with someone the genius of you that you are unwilling and too afraid to share with the world. Find this genus gift and share it today.

There is no reason to leave your gifts and your genius unclaimed at the station. You need to own them and share them with another, even if you need a moment of encouragement, about the truth of who you are.

One thing you should never deny is the truth of who you are.

Your inner beauty awaits in your most beautiful heart to be shared like the precious gift that it is and you are.

Your inner beauty always outshines your outer beauty in every situation.

It's a good time to open to the knowing that that is true.

Blessings be at the gate for you.

True love is who you are in every way possible.

Until next time.

Your friend, Mikela

MESSAGE #46
Will You Invite It In?

Dear Love,
What would you have me know today?

Dearest Otto,

What a gift you are when you show up fully, completely, and full of the wisdom not yet realized by the masses.

What could ever be more fun than rocking the world in your brilliance that you like to hide from us all?

What we would have you know today is how tragic it is that you see other people in your world who, in truth, are equal to you, but certainly not less than or greater than you.

It's waking up inside you, but you are doing your best to fight it.

Do not stop yourself from fully expressing your greatness.

Do not stop yourself from owning the truth of who you are.

Do not put yourself in a box and tape the lid shut with you inside.

Do not worry about anything.

Anything that is not made of love and not made of spiritual and love energy is not worth a moment's time and a moment's focus.

Let's make a pact. Can we?

Will you start your day and end your day in the silence of gratitude and the witnessing of the gift that you are instead of the gift you lay claim to that you truthfully are not.

Remember, who you are is the one who loves himself and loves others and finds unique ways to guide his brothers and sisters home.

You can not do that in doubt, in fear, and in hesitation.

Open your heart, open your mind, and open, if need be, your wallet.

Look at your bad habits as things that are passing in the night and your good habits and your good intentions that are both expressed and unexpressed as what just hasn't found its right timing yet.

We say this because anything that has been a barrier to the truth of who you are, in this day, in this week, in this year, and in this lifetime, should be let go, forgiven, and allowed to reside in the past.

No sense rehashing the painful past memories any more.

The magic cannot happen and the bounty cannot be served if you are not willing to look past all your fears, doubts, stories of the past regrets and past failures, and just say a big fat juicy YES to the life and the future that beckons you, beginning in this moment.

One day you will not have a single worry or a single care about anything that is not founded and kept in the solidness of who you really are when there's nothing left to accept except the beautiful perfection that you are that will live on forever and can never fade away and can never pass away.

If there is any part of you that believes, truly believes, that you are eternal, then don't wait to believe that in the future. Find any thimble you can find and scoop up the most you can fit in that thimble and start there and know that that thimbleful will be enough to start the chain of self-love and self-healing needed for your own personal transformation.

Do not wait for anything to be revealed or anything to happen until you claim who you are, what you are, and how you serve.

Start being who you are, what you are, and serving how you are called to serve (but hold back from) right now in the next moment, the next interaction, and the next opportunity that shows itself to you wherever you are and wherever is needed.

It's time for you to serve yourself and serve humanity as both are not incompatible with each other.

For as you love and you serve yourself, you love and serve the world.

The magic is happening now and now and now.

Will you invite it in?

With complete love for you, my brother.

Mikela

MESSAGE #47
Test this Out

Dear Love,
What would you have me know today?

Dearest Angel Otto,

We come forth to share a moment of love with you and for you, as you are the grand soul that is beyond limitation, without fear, and without anything needed for his journey in the physical and the world beyond all form known to you now.

What we would have you know today is how incumbent it is upon you to lay all your burdens down, lay all your fears (both seen and unseen and unknown) down, and embrace the truth of all things. You are here in a body, in this physical form, to heal, to learn, and to grow and to help as many people as possible do the same in this one beautiful lifetime.

What we would have you know is just how easy it is to metaphorically sharpen the saw indefinitely and not move forward and not honor your path chosen for you and by you. We would also have you know that there is nothing needed that you don't already have to move beyond the beyond and experience a true healing of any and all limitation, beginning right now in this moment.

There is nothing required of you that requires you to be stranded in the muck of limitation. NOTHING.

Once you came here, there were lessons to be learned, healings to take place, memories to be gathered, and memories to be let go of.

Now is the time we request that you open to the one true possibility that you are the one chosen to come forth, at this time, to live as an extension of God's love.

With that being said, we want you to know that the miracle you seek has already been gifted and it is at hand. You are the one. You are the one. You are the one chosen to come forth to experience the love and the beauty, the fears and the doubts, the false and the truth, and everything in between.

There's a letting go that needs to take place within you at this time. The letting go we are insisting happen at this time is the letting go of anything not honoring to the possibilities and the miracles on offer for you or anyone who simply knocks on the door of freedom and requests humbly that a miracle, also known as a shift of perception, take place and that it take place not to release you from any and all thoughts, fears, doubts, or internal hesitations blocking you from claiming your real, true identity as a spirit who loves all things here in a body and is here to learn to live and breathe love.

What can be seen shall be shown now and what can't yet be seen will be seen in the coming days, weeks and months, and then be shown to others who need this simple message of hope, love, and connection with the Divine.

Now we urge you, do not go back to sleep. You are awakening. You are being shown the way and that does NOT include touching any negativity or embracing the insanity of any false thing about who are, what you are, or how you serve.

From here on out, honor the sacred and the Divine in everything and every moment.

Get quiet. Notice your energy and let that be your guide for what to embrace, what to choose, what to say YES to and what to lay down and what to say no to.

Notice your energy and notice what feels good. Move toward what feels good and let go of anything that doesn't have that positive energy attached to it.

One more thing for today.

You don't have to feel miserable, take on regret, shame, or start going down the rabbit hole of feeling less than for anything in your past. The past is complete. It's over. It's history.

It's the result of your best thinking and your best plan you could come up with at any given moment to solve a problem or try to make your life work better.

Take this message to heart.

Love yourself no matter what has happened in the past no matter how much you think you screwed up, or how much you didn't deserve something you consider bad that happened to you.

Check in with yourself and test this out for yourself by simply asking yourself:

"Am I ok in this moment?"

If you don't drag the fears and the thinking about the past or past mistakes in the present moment, you'll see without a shadow of a doubt that not only are you ok but you are perfectly fine.

With deep love and appreciation for you always.

Until we speak again, be well.

Mikela

MESSAGE #48

A Beautiful and Sacred Act

Dear Love,
What would you have me know about surrender?

Dearest Otto,

Waking up is what we see you doing each and every day and we are so happy to see the seismic shifts happening to you and inside you. This is a real blessing to you and to humanity and we congratulate you for who you are being and who you are becoming.

What is this thing surrender?

What we would have you know about surrender is how helpful and valuable it is to surrender to the mystery of life and to surrender to the golden time we now find ourselves in.

Buckle up. The ride is accelerating and the road may get a little bumpy, but that is "normal" and to be expected with all that is on offer for you and your brothers and sisters in the flesh and spirit at this time.

It's time to call off the dogs and stop going in circles because now is the time you can open to the true meaning of all things and we will kindly suggest that the path of surrender that you have flirted with from time to time is here for the major highway to the

Divine inside you. There are many things and ways of being that could potentially have you cross the road and see the blind spots you have before you. You can get any block to a more wonderful life out of the way MUCH quicker and much more in alignment with your true pathway If and that's a big IF you would only surrender to the doorway and the path being offered by the great one, the one who is the lead agent and the leader and creator of all things.

Surrender is NOT based on helplessness and hopelessness. Quite the opposite. Surrender is the most beautiful and sacred act of a lifetime.

Freedom, one would think, is about doing what you want and opening the doorway to the Divine by doing whatever you want, but that's not the best part of surrender.

The best part of surrender is the fact that as you surrender, you give up the desire for drama, pain, and holding on.

Surrender is the choice to BE in an open and willing space where no one and no thing could ever stand in your way or open to any sort of judgment that prevents you or anyone from opening to their highest version of themselves and their highest calling. This is because they are not surrendering to something unseen, something painful, or something that doesn't allow them to open.

Surrendering in its highest form is surrendering to the Divine and not just to the big, grey-bearded white man in the sky, but instead surrendering to the wisdom in yourself and the desires that come from some other place than the personality where desires are all ego and fear-based.

Surrender in its simplest form is what is called for when you release the idea of doing things "your way" and seeing the logic and importance of surrendering to what is most desired and most needed at the heart, mind, and soul level.

True surrender means you have decided to listen, truly listen, to that "small, still voice within" as the mystics say and live your life from that point of light or attraction.

Surrender is the act of trusting in something greater than you about what is best, what is needed, and what is your next right action.

But all this surrendering isn't just about doing something to make this feel alright, whatever the this is for you in the moment.

Surrendering is the requirement we all go through to give up struggle and give up our way of seeing life, seeing another, or seeing a situation in favor of something akin to a grand or Divine plan or act for you and only you.

In the act of surrendering, there is not one way that is good for you and the same act that is also good for your brothers and sisters.

Everyone born into this time and space will have a different place to surrender from and to.

This is true.

What is also true is the fact that in surrendering, you are surrendering to a higher way and not a lower way or a way incongruent with your path of harmony and growth.

Surrendering is not a path to be feared or thinking you have to give up something or some part of you. It is indeed the kindest and most sacred act of a lifetime, the act of saying YES to and living into ALL of who you truly are.

It is a sacred "power move" that propels you into the light where your path can and will be fully illuminated and shown to you as a guide for what will most serve your highest good next.

Surrender is a choice and it is an internal choice for love and for loving yourself.

Surrender is NOT a giving up.

It is a moving toward the Divine and the Divine in you.

This owning, saying YES to and this internal loving that comes as you embrace true, loving surrender, will indeed change you but it won't change you in ways that you fear.

This true surrender of the heart and soul is an act of bringing your possibilities closer and closer to you in real time.

This surrender is borne of love and the letting go of whatever your personality is holding onto that keeps you stuck in an idea or a certain way of seeing life.

Surrender is never a bad thing. Surrender is always and only a surrendering to the truth of what is.

And that is pure potential and pure possibility in this moment and in this one sacred life that is never ending.

Blessings be to you, my friend.

Until next time.

Mikela

MESSAGE #49

The Right Timing

Dear Love,
What would you have me know today?

Dearest Otto,

We are loving you so much in this moment for who you are and what you are and that is a beautiful soul sent here to love and be loved, to believe in himself without any real reason to believe in himself other than he just is and to live in perfect harmony with the rules of nature.

What we would have you know today is about the idea of moving forward toward the creation of what is wanted vs the slowing down and reverting to the past ways, past hurts, past things, and ways of being that no longer make sense when looked upon from the eyes and spirit of the beloved.

One thing you can say for sure is it is time to wake up, open your arms, and wait for the crossroads to appear, if it hasn't already, and see that crossroads as a pathway to the decisions in this moment and in this time as sacred instructions from the Divine.

You never want to look for the freedom in something that can't offer you the freedom you seek. But you most definitely DO want to open to the gifts that are already here inside you in full bloom waiting for the perfect timing to be made manifest.

Here's how you know something is in its perfect timing in your life:

It is happening in the here and now.

If something is NOT present in the here and now, there is simply no way it can NOT be in its perfect timing. It's just not possible.

You can hope for it, pray for it, wish for it, and for heaven's sake, if it's not happening now, it's not the perfect timing.

If it's not happening, it may not be the right way, in connection with the right person, the right timing or may not be possible FOR YOU in this lifetime.

"Right timing" is a shortcut for the timing you want, you think you need, and the timing you desire for something you think would add something to your life.

Believe us when we say, there is nothing that could be added to your life that could bring any value that is not already here.

This is not a joke.

It's not funny.

But the fun part of this is about what it means to be in true and total surrender.

True and total surrender is a rarity these days and that's the problem you and your brothers and sisters see on a regular basis. True and total surrender is the package that gets accepted with the things you call the wrong "stuff" in them, but there can be no such thing as the "wrong stuff."

Walking hand in hand and arm in arm in surrender is just one of the many doorways you can open to the higher realms and the higher self, known as the Divine.

Nowhere does it ever say in the "good book" that you have to do everything yourself in order to make a life truly work out.

But it does say that the Divine is already in you.

Rarely, and we do mean rarely, do you ever get a second chance in life but this moment is different. This time, there are no more soldiers waiting to take you home.

Listen up, my dear friend, cast all your burdens to the wayside and offer up a solid line to not go over.

For the "right timing" will never appear as long as there is any energy blocking the energetic path for the manifestation you are wanting.

Once there was a small woman waiting at the market for a ride but there was no ride. She was waiting and waiting and still no ride. The perfect timing had not yet arrived for this woman.

What a difference an insight can make toward the fulfillment of a wine gone stale.

Come forth now and partake of the wisdom that is being offered to take the train and go once and for all where no other named you has gone before.

If you tune in and get the insight that it's time to speed up, then it is time to speed up. What you always want to do is listen to the deeper calm voice that shares with you the wisdom from the tree of wisdom and speak to the others and beg them to come in and celebrate the loveliness of a life well-lived.

Try it, whatever it is, and the revealing of what is inside will surely appear.

No more waiting for something needed to appear. The waiting is over.

One true test is all it takes to know, truly know, what is in the way of your own greatness.

And, what is in the way is nothing.

Nothing is ever in the way of wanting something to manifest whose time has come.

The manifestation is actually "on the way."

It's in the doorway right now, waiting for the right opportunity to be welcomed in and the best part is simply this:

All manifestation is always "on the way."

The only thing that can ever stop it is two things:

1) Your negative or stinking thinking that is already ready to shift

2) God's timing just hasn't happened YET.

We simply urge you to wipeout anything and everything from your consciousness that could possibly hinder the transmission of energy to its rightful place.

Share love with every one you see before you on this day.

Blessings be.

Your Friend,

Mikela

MESSAGE #50

Loving Yourself

Dear love,
What would you have me know today about loving myself?

Dearest Otto,

We so love you and we only want the best and the highest for you, and we so appreciate you and your commitment to these times of asking and being willing to listen.

We thank you for who you are and who you are showing up as in this world. You are a blessing. Thank you.

What we would have you know today about loving yourself is that this is the most natural thing in the world that almost everyone rejects.

Loving yourself is the kindest, the most beautiful, the most extraordinary thing you can do for yourself, for the people in your life, and for the entire universe.

As you love yourself, you are making a seemingly bold stand, but it really isn't.

All you are doing when you are loving yourself is you are acknowledging the truth of what is.

You are a child of the Creator and let's not get bogged down in the names that people assigned to the Creator because the names people assign to the Creator is where it gets murky, fuzzy and painful for people.

So, if we simply said the Creator loves you and it's okay for you to love you, then bit by bit all the drama, all the misunderstandings, and all the reasons why it's not okay for you to love yourself fade away bit by bit.

One of the things we would have you know about loving yourself is how important it is.

If there's any creating that you want to do in this world, anything that you believe that would make for a wonderful life, everything in those realms are benefited when you show up and love yourself more, then a little more, and then a little more after that.

The only thing that ever gets in the way of someone loving themselves is a story that it's not okay to do that, that they are somehow flawed in some way, and that we don't deserve or we shouldn't be loved and that is so far from the truth.

Every single person who has ever lived, regardless of what they've done, all deserve to be loved and not because of something that a person does.

Every single human alive and every single human who has ever existed deserves to be loved just for the sake that they exist.

That's it.

They exist and the very fact that they exist qualifies them immediately to be loved, to be honored, and to be embraced by the Divine and by themselves.

There is no place and no room for pain, agony, self-doubt, and self-hatred when what is really on offer is embracing you and all that you are.

Otto, we have said that you are a soul in a body that loves himself and loves others and we are commanding you to do that until the Spirit says "times up," and we're serious about that.

Love yourself and love others until the Spirit says times up.

What we would have you do is to show up in your moments and when the doubts appear, cast them by the side as if they were something to be discarded like they are unimportant, because your doubts are always unimportant.

Your misunderstandings of who you are truly are unimportant.

The only thing that is important is that you recognize the truth of all truths.

And that is that you are a piece of the Divine in action in this lifetime, in this body, in this spirit, as the soul that you truly are.

There is no time and no room for doubting the truth of who you are.

Love yourself.

Those are the only instructions there are.

There is no doing that is ever needed to love yourself.

You simply love yourself because you exist, not because of anything you do in the world.

Anything you do in the world is just simply anything you do in the world.

It does not define you.

It does not make up who you are.

It does not make you better or worse than another human.

Your only job is to love yourself and love others until time is up.

Thank you for listening.

We love you and we thank you for attending to these sacred times with us.

Your friend in the spirit world,

Mikela

Acknowledgements

To bring *Messages from Mikela* into the world has been such an amazing gift that has touched, moved, and changed me at so many levels. And for that I am eternally grateful.

I first want to acknowledge Elizabeth Gilbert for going on the Tim Ferriss podcast in early October 2024, describing her practice of the "Two-way Prayer," and for changing my life.

Liz, there was something about the way you described its impact on you and your life that instantly made me say to myself, "Yes, I'm going to do that." The impact of the "Two-way Prayer," as you described it, in my life simply cannot be measured. My starting to do "Two-way Prayers" is where the messages in this book came from and I am grateful to you for your spiritual guidance from a distance. Thank you.

To Deryl Sweeney, Igor Furdik, and Fiona Ross: Your support and encouragement to keep going and share the "Messages from Mikela" to a wider audience and not just keep them for myself was incredibly valuable in deciding to publish this book and allow these messages to serve others in deeper and deeper ways. Thank you. I love you.

To Susie Collins: You are my love, my best friend, my spiritual partner and business partner. Your gifts as a collaborator, as an organizer, and an encourager are amazing. Words cannot describe the love and gratitude I have for you and who you are to me. Without you and your contributions to this book, there's no book. You truly are incredible. Thank you.

To Mikela (and the gang as coined by Deryl Sweeny): Thank you for your words, your gifts, and your love. You have loved me, cared for me, and you have rocked me and changed me to my core. Your influence on me and my life is mind-blowing to say the least. I am certain your words in the book are going to change the lives of many. Thank you for who you have been to me and to countless others. I am grateful and I am blessed to have you in my life. I love you.

And finally, to you the reader: I want to acknowledge you for being willing to read a book like this and opening yourself to new possibilities and new ways of being in the world. Always remember, you are more amazing than you know. My desire is for the words in this book to help you see that at deeper and deeper levels.

About the Author

Otto Collins is a relationship and life coach, author, speaker, spiritual teacher, seminar leader, businessman, and spiritual seeker who spends his time helping men and women all over the world see the truth about who they truly are and helps them to create the life they truly want from that place of abundance and possibility.

Along with his wife, Susie, he is the co-author of over a dozen books and programs on love, relationships, and personal and spiritual growth, including BIG FAT LOVE: *The Book of Possibilities* and *Preaching to Monkeys: Hope, Healing and Understanding for Fathers, Sons, and the People Who Love Them.*

Otto began receiving the first "Messages From Mikela" in Early October 2024.

To sign up for a one-on-one private coaching conversation with Otto or to learn about his other books, audios, videos, coaching, consulting, seminars, classes, media appearances and everything else he's up to in the world, you can find him on most social media outlets or by visiting OttoCollins.com or SusieandOtto.com

Contact info:
You can find Otto on Facebook and Instagram or
OttoCollins.com and SusieandOtto.com

www.ingramcontent.com/pod-product-compliance
Lightning Source LLC
LaVergne TN
LVHW051511080426
835509LV00017B/2032